HISTORIANS AT WORK

What Did the Internment of Japanese Americans Mean?

Readings Selected and Introduced by

Alice Yang Murray

University of California, Santa Cruz

Selections by

Roger Daniels

Peter Irons

Michi Weglyn

Gary Y. Okihiro

Valerie J. Matsumoto

Bedford / St. Martin's   *Boston* ♦ *New York*

For Bedford/St. Martin's

Executive Editor for History and Political Science: Katherine E. Kurzman
Developmental Editor: Mary T. Stone
Senior Production Supervisor: Dennis Conroy
Marketing Manager: Charles Cavaliere
Project Management: Books By Design, Inc.
Text Design: Claire Seng-Niemoeller
Cover Design: Zenobia Rivetna
Cover Art: Eviction Order. Detailed instructions on eviction procedures. Posted
  in San Francisco, CA, April 1, 1942. Authorized by Executive Order #9066.
  Courtesy of the National Japanese American Historical Society.
  Evacuation Day. Mother and child en route to detention camp. Bainbridge
  Island, Washington, March 30, 1942. National Japanese American Historical
  Society archive, courtesy of the Museum of History and Industry, Seattle,
  Washington.
Composition: G&S Typesetters, Inc.
Printing and Binding: Haddon Craftsmen, an R. R. Donnelley & Sons Company

President: Charles H. Christensen
Editorial Director: Joan E. Feinberg
Director of Marketing: Karen R. Melton
Director of Editing, Design, and Production: Marcia Cohen
Manager, Publishing Services: Emily Berleth

Library of Congress Catalog Card Number: 99-63689

Copyright © 2000 by Bedford/St. Martin's

Manufactured in the United States of America.

5 4 3 2 1 0
f e d c b a

For information, write: Bedford/St. Martin's, 75 Arlington Street, Boston, MA 02116
(617-399-4000)

ISBN: 0-312-20829-4 (paperback)
      0-312-22816-3 (hardcover)

Acknowledgments

Acnowledgments and copyrights are continued at the back of the book on page
  163, which constitutes an extension of the copyright page.
Map of Assembly and Relocation Centers, from *Years of Infamy: The Untold Story
  of America's Concentration Camps* (New York: Morrow Quill Paperbacks, 1976), 6.
  Reprinted with permission from the California State Polytechnic University,
  Pomona, which has established the Michi and Walter Weglyn Chair for
  Multicultural Studies to honor the memory of Michi and Walter Weglyn and
  their dedicated efforts to seek justice for all persons of Japanese ancestry who
  were unjustly incarcerated during World War II.

Foreword

The short, inexpensive, and tightly focused books in the Historians at Work series set out to show students what historians do by turning closed specialist debate into an open discussion about important and interesting historical problems. These volumes invite students to confront the issues historians grapple with while providing enough support so that students can form their own opinions and join the debate. The books convey the intellectual excitement of "doing history" that should be at the core of any undergraduate study of the discipline. Each volume starts with a contemporary historical question that is posed in the book's title. The question focuses on either an important historical document (the Declaration of Independence, the Emancipation Proclamation) or a major problem or event (the beginnings of American slavery, the Pueblo Revolt of 1680) in American history. An introduction supplies the basic historical context students need and then traces the ongoing debate among historians, showing both how old questions have yielded new answers and how new questions have arisen. Following this two-part introduction are four to six interpretive selections by top scholars, reprinted in their entirety from journals and books, including endnotes. Each selection is either a very recent piece or a classic argument that is still in play and is headed by a question that relates it to the book's core problem. Volumes that focus on a document reprint it in the opening materials so that students can read arguments alongside the evidence and reasoning on which they rest.

One purpose of these books is to show students that they *can* engage with sophisticated writing and arguments. To help them do so, each selection includes apparatus that provides context for engaged reading and critical thinking. An informative headnote introduces the angle of inquiry that the reading explores and closes with Questions for a Closer Reading, which invite students to probe the selection's assumptions, evidence, and argument. At the end of the book, Making Connections questions offer students ways to read the essays against one another, showing how interesting problems emerge from the debate. Suggestions for Further Reading conclude each book, pointing interested students toward relevant materials for extended study.

Historical discourse is rarely a matter of simple opposition. These volumes show how ideas develop and how answers change, as minor themes turn into major considerations. The Historians at Work volumes bring together thoughtful statements in an ongoing conversation about topics that continue to engender debate, drawing students into the historical discussion with enough context and support to participate themselves. These books aim to show how serious scholars have made sense of the past and why what they do is both enjoyable and worthwhile.

EDWARD COUNTRYMAN

Preface

On October 9, 1990, Attorney General Richard Thornburgh presented an official government apology to Mamoru Eto, a Japanese American who was interned during World War II. In 1942, Eto was one of 120,000 Japanese Americans uprooted from their homes and incarcerated behind barbed wire. In 1990, the wheelchair-bound 107-year-old traveled from a Los Angeles nursing home to Washington, D.C., to become the first recipient of a payment from a federal redress program. "By finally admitting a wrong," Thornburgh told Eto and the eight other elderly internees who were present, "a nation does not destroy its integrity but, rather, reinforces the sincerity of its commitment to the Constitution and hence to its people." The attorney general then handed each of them a check for $20,000. In a written statement accompanying all redress payments, President George Bush declared, "We can never fully right the wrongs of the past, but we can take a clear stand for justice and recognize that serious injustices were done to Japanese Americans during World War II."

Although many factors contributed to the government's recognition in 1990 of the injustice of internment, historical research played a major role. In fact, the first three authors in this collection were important activists in the redress movement of the 1970s and 1980s. Roger Daniels, Peter Irons, and Michi Weglyn testified before the government and spoke to Japanese American community groups to mobilize support for redress. In their published work and public appearances, these scholars challenged America's heroic image during World War II by denouncing the rationale for internment and describing internees' suffering during and after the war. In these accounts, the government's decision to intern Japanese Americans, two-thirds of whom were American-born citizens, could not be justified or excused as a tragic mistake caused by wartime hysteria. Using a variety of government sources, including newly declassified documents, these scholars revealed in great detail how the advocates of internment were influenced by racism, greed, and political expediency.

As researchers and activists, Daniels, Irons, and Weglyn changed American history. They not only provided evidence for redress lobbyists, but they also took part in the campaign. They helped convince politicians, judges, and the press to acknowledge the injustice of internment. Perhaps most important, however, was their impact on the Japanese American community. For decades after the war, many former internees repressed memories of the war because they blamed themselves for the incarceration. By indicting the motives and policies of the architects of internment, these scholars encouraged former internees to shift the burden of guilt from themselves to the government, to remember what happened during the war, and to share those memories with the public. In other words, these historians not only transformed views of the causes of internment, they also changed the understanding of the consequences of the incarceration. There was a "snowball" effect as former internees who heard others recount life behind barbed wire decided to describe their own painful experiences. Increasing numbers of former internees began demanding redress and helped sustain the movement in the 1980s.

The redress movement in turn helped create new sources on the history of Japanese American responses to internment. The final two selections in this collection, by Gary Y. Okihiro and Valerie Matsumoto, provide further evidence of the relationship between history, politics, and scholarship. When Okihiro tried to research a history of resistance in the camps in the 1970s, he had to reinterpret government sources because few former internees were willing to talk with researchers about the war. Because of the redress movement, more Japanese Americans became comfortable speaking about their experiences and working with oral historians. In fact, Valerie Matsumoto began her research at the behest of a community in California that wanted to preserve a record of its history. These two selections illustrate how a critical reexamination of wartime sources and the collection of recent oral history sources can shed new light on the diversity of Japanese American experiences in the internment camps.

The design of this book reflects two considerations. First, I want to provide students with a wide range of influential scholarship on the causes and consequences of internment. Students can use this collection to compare the sources, methods, and interpretations of researchers in the fields of political, constitutional, cultural, and social history. Second, I wish to draw students' attention to the process of producing historical research and knowledge. The introduction to each selection discusses the background and perspectives of the author to help students think about how the researcher's intellectual, social, and political commitments might have shaped his or her views of the past and approach to the study of internment. I hope that this will encourage students to contemplate the relationship between politics and scholarship and to explore connections between intellectual agendas, scholarly careers, and political activism.

Acknowledgments

I am grateful to Jack N. Rakove for suggesting that I do this volume and to Katherine E. Kurzman, Bedford/St. Martin's executive editor for history and political science, for recognizing the importance of including internment in the Historians at Work series. Katherine and developmental editor Mary T. Stone provided encouragement and unfailing support as I completed the manuscript. I appreciate the professionalism and commitment of the entire staff at Bedford/St. Martin's: publisher Charles H. Christensen, associate publisher Joan E. Feinberg, managing editor Emily Berleth, art director Donna Dennison, and Books By Design coordinator Nancy Benjamin. I was able to interview many of the historians in this collection because of a grant from the Civil Liberties Public Education Fund. Many historians also gave generous and perceptive advice on the book. My sincere thanks to John Cheng, Karen Dunn-Haley, Ariela Gross, Leslie Harris, Brian Hayashi, Victor Jew, Renee Romano, Wendy Wall, and Jun Xing for helping me develop my prospectus for the book. The manuscript benefited greatly from the insightful suggestions of Donald Collins, Arthur A. Hansen, Victor Jew, Wendy Kozol, K. Scott Wong, and two anonymous readers. Their questions and comments were invaluable in improving the final manuscript. Donald Collins deserves special mention for allowing me to use his copies of negatives of several photos from the National Archives. Roger Daniels and Gary Okihiro granted me permission to reprint their scholarship without a fee and took the time to review my description of their lives. I am truly grateful to have had the support and assistance of so many professional colleagues. Finally, I thank Steve Murray and David Yang-Murray for their love and moral support as I completed this book.

ALICE YANG MURRAY

A Note for Students

Every piece of written history starts when somebody becomes curious and asks questions. The very first problem is who, or what, to study. A historian might ask an old question yet again, after deciding that existing answers are not good enough. But brand-new questions can emerge about old, familiar topics, particularly in light of new findings or directions in research, such as the rise of women's history in the late 1970s.

In one sense history is all that happened in the past. In another it is the universe of potential evidence that the past has bequeathed. But written history does not exist until a historian collects and probes that evidence (*research*), makes sense of it (*interpretation*), and shows to others what he or she has seen so that they can see it too (*writing*). Good history begins with respecting people's complexity, not with any kind of preordained certainty. It might well mean using modern techniques that were unknown at the time, such as Freudian psychology or statistical assessment by computer. But good historians always approach the past on its own terms, taking careful stock of the period's cultural norms and people's assumptions or expectations, no matter how different from contemporary attitudes. Even a few decades can offer a surprisingly large gap to bridge, as each generation discovers when it evaluates the accomplishments of those who have come before.

To write history well requires three qualities. One is the courage to try to understand people whom we never can meet — unless our subject is very recent — and to explain events that no one can re-create. The second quality is the humility to realize that we can never entirely appreciate either the people or the events under study. However much evidence is compiled and however smart the questions posed, the past remains too large to contain. It will always continue to surprise.

The third quality historians need is the curiosity that turns sterile facts into clues about a world that once was just as alive, passionate, frightening, and exciting as our own, yet in different ways. Today we know how past events "turned out." But the people taking part had no such knowledge. Good history recaptures those people's fears, hopes, frustrations, failures, and achievements; it tells about people who faced the predicaments and choices that still confront us as we begin the twenty-first century.

All the essays collected in this volume bear on a single, shared problem that the authors agree is important, however differently they may choose to respond to it. On its own, each essay reveals a fine mind coming to grips with a worthwhile question. Taken together, the essays give a sense of just how complex the human situation can be. That point — that human situations are complex — applies just as much to life today as to the lives led in the past. History has no absolute "lessons" to teach; it follows no invariable "laws." But knowing about another time might be of some help as we struggle to live within our own.

EDWARD COUNTRYMAN

Contents

coram nobis, available only to criminal defendants whose trials had been tainted by 'fundamental error' or 'manifest injustice.'"

Michi Weglyn

Hostages

"The removals in the United States were only a part of forced uprootings which occurred almost simultaneously in Alaska, Canada, Mexico, Central America, parts of South America, and the Caribbean island of Haiti and the Dominican Republic."

Gary Y. Okihiro

Tule Lake under Martial Law: A Study in Japanese Resistance

"In contrast, it can be seen that there had been a history of resistance and there was no such dramatic break, because both groups, for and against status quo, were committed to a program of reform and the continuing fight for a recognition of their humanity."

Valerie J. Matsumoto

Amache

"They were sustained through this period by deep-rooted networks of relatives and friends, and they maintained family bonds even though many journeyed farther from home than ever before."

PART ONE

Introduction

The Internment of Japanese Americans

The Internment of Japanese Americans

From Pearl Harbor to Mass Incarceration:
A Brief Narrative

On the morning of December 7, 1941, Japanese Americans learned the shocking news that Japan had attacked Pearl Harbor in Hawaii. Like most Americans, they were stunned by the surprise assault that destroyed America's Pacific fleet. As Americans of Japanese ancestry, however, these immigrants and their children, American citizens by virtue of their birth in the United States, also feared retaliation. Even before the smoke had cleared from the ruins at Pearl Harbor, Federal Bureau of Investigation agents began rounding up suspected "enemy aliens" throughout Hawaii and the West Coast. Most of those arrested were male immigrants put under surveillance a year before the attack because they were leaders of the ethnic community—Japanese Association officials, Buddhist priests, Japanese-language teachers, and newspaper editors. In the weeks following the declaration of war, the FBI arrested more than two thousand of these Japanese immigrants and ten thousand immigrants from Germany and Italy suspected of belonging to pro-Nazi or fascist organizations.

The FBI interrogated these immigrants and sent those considered "dangerous" to internment camps administered by the Department of Justice in places such as Santa Fe, New Mexico; Bismarck, North Dakota; and Missoula, Montana (see map). By February 16, 1942, the Justice Department camps held 2,192 Japanese, 1,393 German, and 264 Italian "enemy aliens." The largest of these camps, the one in Crystal City, Texas, also interned many of the 2,264 Japanese Latin Americans deported from their countries so that the United States might exchange them for Americans held by Japan in 1942 and 1943.

The Justice Department camps held about 10 percent of all Japanese immigrants from the West Coast. Many of these immigrants questioned the fairness of their hearings. Masuo Yasui, for example, was interned for subversion because he could not "prove" to the government prosecutor at Fort Missoula that one of his children's homework assignments, which included

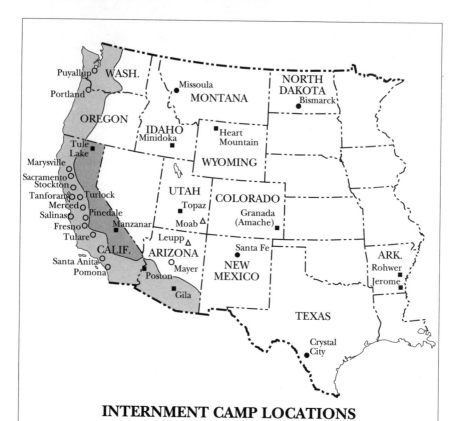

INTERNMENT CAMP LOCATIONS

○ **ASSEMBLY CENTERS**

Puyallup, Wash.
Portland, Ore.
Marysville, Calif.
Sacramento, Calif.
Tanforan, Calif.
Stockton, Calif.
Turlock, Calif.
Merced, Calif.
Pinedale, Calif.
Salinas, Calif.
Fresno, Calif.
Tulare, Calif.
Santa Anita, Calif.
Pomona, Calif.
Mayer, Ariz.

● **JUSTICE DEPARTMENT INTERNMENT CAMPS**

Santa Fe, N. Mex.
Bismarck, N. Dak.
Crystal City, Tex.
Missoula, Mont.

△ **CITIZEN ISOLATION CAMPS**

Moab, Utah
Leupp, Ariz.

■ **RELOCATION CENTERS**

Manzanar, Calif.
Tule Lake, Calif.
Poston, Ariz.
Gila, Ariz.
Minidoka, Ida.
Heart Mountain, Wyo.
Granada, Colo.
Topaz, Utah
Rohwer, Ark.
Jerome, Ark.

| | Military Area 1, West Coast |
| Military Area 2 or "Free Zone" until March 29, 1942 |

Map of internment camp locations. Courtesy Michi Weglyn, *Years of Infamy: The Untold Story of America's Concentration Camps.*

a drawing of the Panama Canal, was not evidence of his plans to blow up the canal. Wishing to return to their families, these men tried to convince the authorities that they were no threat to the war effort. All hopes of returning home, however, were dashed when they learned in March 1942 that all Japanese Americans on the West Coast would be interned in separate camps run by the War Relocation Authority (WRA).

Ultimately, 120,000 Japanese Americans, two-thirds of whom were citizens, were interned in one of ten WRA camps (see map). Why did the U.S. government decide to remove and confine people from the West Coast solely on the basis of their Japanese ancestry? Most scholars now agree that this decision was not simply the product of wartime hysteria but reflected a long history of anti-Japanese hostility fueled by economic competition and racial stereotypes. In fact, any menace posed by the Axis was much stronger on the East Coast than on the West Coast throughout 1942. Along the Atlantic coast, German submarines regularly torpedoed unconvoyed American ships. Thirteen ships were sunk in the last weeks of January and nearly sixty vessels were lost in the North Atlantic and along the eastern seaboard. By contrast, the West Coast did not suffer any attacks from the Japanese until after President Franklin Delano Roosevelt issued Executive Order 9066, authorizing the removal of Japanese Americans from the West Coast, on February 19, 1942. Four days after the order was announced, a Japanese submarine lobbed a few shells at a Santa Barbara oil field, and on September 9 a Japanese seaplane dropped two incendiary bombs on the Siskiyou National Forest in Oregon. Both of these incidents, which caused little damage and no injuries, occurred after government officials had already decided to uproot Japanese Americans from their homes and communities.

Of course, the Germans had not attacked Pearl Harbor. Yet even though many advocates of internment falsely claimed that Hawaii was full of "Jap spies and saboteurs," there was no mass removal or incarceration of people of Japanese ancestry on the islands. Why, then, did officials decide to intern all Japanese Americans living on the West Coast? Historians now emphasize the role of a century-long campaign against Asian immigrants. Anti-Asian activists, who had first mobilized against Chinese immigrants when they began arriving in California in the 1840s, employed the same "yellow peril" imagery to attack Japanese immigrants in the late nineteenth century. Japanese immigrant men were portrayed as spies, sex fiends, or cheap laborers undermining the ability of white workingmen to earn a living. Japanese immigrant women were accused of "breeding like rats" and producing "unassimilable" children, who were then forced to attend segregated schools. Envious of the success of immigrant farmers, the anti-Japanese forces persuaded several western states, beginning with California in 1913, to pass "alien land laws" denying Japanese immigrants the right to own land. In 1922, the U.S. Supreme Court ruled in *Ozawa v. U.S.* that Japanese immigrants could not become naturalized American citizens. Two years later, anti-Japanese politicians convinced Congress to terminate all immigration from Japan. The Immigration Act of 1924 was also supported by many groups wanting quotas to restrict immigration from southern and eastern Europe. Anti-Japanese exclusionists, however, made sure this legislation denied Japan even a token quota that would have allowed the entry of no more than a couple of hundred immigrants each year.

The attack on Pearl Harbor and the rapid succession of victories by Japanese forces in the Pacific rekindled the embers of anti-Japanese sentiment. On December 7, 1941, the same day as the bombing of Pearl Harbor, Japan struck the Malay Peninsula, Hong Kong, Wake and Midway Islands, and the Philippines. The Japanese invaded Thailand the next day. Guam fell on December 13, Wake Island on December 24, and Hong Kong on December 25. American forces had to abandon Manila, the capital of the Philippines, on December 27 and retreat to the Bataan peninsula.

As Americans struggled to make sense of these losses, news accounts of the attack on Pearl Harbor fanned the flames of hatred against Japanese Americans. Secretary of the Navy Frank Knox told the press of an effective "fifth column"* in Hawaii, even though his official report contained no such charges. The report remained classified, and the government did nothing to allay the fears spawned by Knox's remarks as headlines blared "Secretary of Navy Blames Fifth Column for the Raid" and "Fifth Column Treachery Told." Further misleading the public and contributing to the "official" validation of sabotage suspicions were declarations by a committee of inquiry on Pearl Harbor, led by Supreme Court Justice Owen J. Roberts, that Japanese spies had helped the enemy during the "sneak" attack. Newspapers began reporting wild rumors about the bombing of Pearl Harbor as "facts." The *Los Angeles Times,* for example, announced that Japanese fliers shot down over Pearl Harbor were wearing class rings of the University of Hawaii and Honolulu High School. The paper even claimed that a Japanese resident painted himself green and "camouflaged himself so he could hide in the foliage and aid attacking Japs."

As reports of Pearl Harbor "treachery" proliferated, West Coast politicians stoked the fires of anti-Japanese prejudice and began clamoring for the removal of Japanese immigrants and citizens. In California, Congressman Leland Ford, Mayor Fletcher Bowron of Los Angeles, Governor Culbert Olson, and California Attorney General Earl Warren demanded that Washington take action to protect the West Coast from "Jap" spies. The advocates of internment found a receptive audience in the commander of the Western Defense Command, Lieutenant General John L. DeWitt. In

---

fifth column: a covert group or faction of subversive agents.

charge of protecting West Coast security, DeWitt was more impressed by the dire warnings of California politicians and Allen Gullion, provost marshall general for the army, than by reports from Naval Intelligence, the FBI, and the Army General Staff dismissing any threat of sabotage, espionage, or invasion.

On February 14, 1942, DeWitt sent a memo to Secretary of War Henry Stimson recommending the removal of all immigrants and citizens of Japanese ancestry from the West Coast. DeWitt's memo declared, "The Japanese race is an enemy race," and "racial affinities are not severed by migration." Even second- and third-generation Japanese Americans who were citizens and "Americanized" could not be trusted, according to DeWitt, because "the racial strains are undiluted." Taking for granted that all "Japs" were disloyal, DeWitt concluded that the "very fact that no sabotage has taken place to date" was a "disturbing and confirming indication that such action will be taken."

Why did Washington accept DeWitt's recommendation? Members of the government who knew there was no need to remove Japanese Americans mounted a tepid response to the advocates of internment. FBI director J. Edgar Hoover wrote a memo to Attorney General Francis Biddle noting that the public hysteria was groundless. Biddle argued against mass exclusion at a luncheon conference with President Roosevelt. But neither one publicized their objections or criticized plans for mass removal on constitutional grounds. Once it became clear that the War Department and the president supported DeWitt's request, Biddle even proceeded to help implement the plans for mass removal.

President Roosevelt accepted Secretary of War Stimson's advice to endorse DeWitt's plans and ignored the advice of his own intelligence specialists. Roosevelt, along with the War Department and the Western Defense Command, had received a series of reports from Curtis Munson* based on information from the Honolulu FBI, British Intelligence in California, and Naval Intelligence in southern California. "For the most part," Munson wrote, "the local Japanese are loyal to the United States, or at worst, hope that by remaining quiet they can avoid concentration camps or irresponsible mobs." Japanese Americans, Munson concluded, were no more likely to be "disloyal than any other racial group in the United States with whom we went to war." Munson not only denounced proposals for mass exclusion but also urged the president or vice president to issue a statement affirming the loyalty of Japanese Americans to calm the hysteria enveloping the West Coast.

Curtis Munson: a successful Chicago businessman who posed as a government official to gather information for Roosevelt's own informal intelligence operation.

Instead, Roosevelt signed Executive Order 9066 on February 19, 1942, authorizing the War Department to designate military areas from which "any and all persons may be excluded." Although this order never specifically named Japanese Americans, it soon became clear that they would be the only group targeted for mass removal. DeWitt also wanted to exclude German and Italian "enemy aliens" from the West Coast, but his civilian superiors at the War Department overruled him. They rejected a blanket removal policy that would have uprooted the immigrant parents of heroes such as Joe DiMaggio and alienated millions of voters of Italian and German ancestry. Japanese Americans, however, lacked such political clout because immigrants could not vote and few second-generation citizens had reached voting age.

Individuals of Japanese ancestry in Hawaii were spared from mass exclusion despite the fact that the islands were more vulnerable to an invasion than the West Coast. The 158,000 people of Japanese ancestry in Hawaii were, however, viewed with suspicion and suffered special restrictions under martial law. "Enemy aliens" in Hawaii were required to carry a registration card at all times and endured travel and work limitations. Almost fifteen hundred "suspects" of Japanese ancestry were arrested and interned in camps run by the U.S. Army or the Department of Justice because of their activities within the ethnic community. Yet General DeWitt's counterpart in Hawaii, General Delos Emmons, recognized that Japanese labor was critical to both the civilian and the military economies of the islands. Japanese Americans made up less than 2 percent of the population of the West Coast and could be removed without much difficulty. But removing more than 35 percent of the population of Hawaii not only would be a logistical nightmare but also would cripple many industries needed for the war effort. In Oahu, 90 percent of the carpenters, almost all of the transportation workers, and a significant proportion of the agricultural laborers were of Japanese ancestry. Thus, although Secretary of the Navy Knox demanded that "all of the Japs" be removed from Oahu and the War Department sent several requests to remove Japanese residents to the mainland, Emmons stalled and ultimately frustrated Washington's calls for mass internment.

DeWitt, by contrast, quickly implemented plans for mass exclusion on the West Coast. At first, he simply ordered Japanese Americans to leave Military Area 1, which consisted of southern Arizona and the western portions of Washington, Oregon, and California (see map). Yet "voluntary evacuation" was short-lived because public officials in the mountain states condemned the prospect of their states becoming "dumping grounds" for California "Japs." If they were too dangerous to roam freely in California, why weren't they too dangerous to let loose in Idaho and Wyoming? With the exception of Governor Ralph Carr of Colorado, the governors of these western states unanimously opposed voluntary migration and urged that Japanese Americans be placed in "concentration camps."

Consequently, at the end of March, "voluntary evacuation" was replaced with what the government called a "planned and systematic evacuation." The government used such euphemisms to mask the fact that immigrants and citizens would be incarcerated behind barbed wire. Even the three thousand Japanese Americans who had moved from Military Area 1 to Military Area 2 in the eastern half of California (see map), based on government assurances that this area would remain a "free zone," were forced into internment camps.

The Internment Camps

The government developed a two-step internment program. Japanese Americans were first transported to one of sixteen "assembly centers" near their homes and then sent to one of ten "relocation centers" in California, Arizona, Utah, Idaho, Wyoming, Colorado, or Arkansas (see map). Most Japanese Americans had less than a week's notice before being uprooted from their homes and community. Instructed to bring only what they could carry, most had little choice but to sell businesses, homes, and prized possessions for a fraction of their value. Internment also disrupted educational and career plans. But for many Japanese Americans, the stigma of suspected disloyalty and the loss of liberty inflicted the deepest wounds. As one internee later recalled, "The most valuable thing I lost was my freedom."

A few Japanese Americans defied DeWitt's orders. Lawyer Minoru Yasui, still outraged by the internment of his father, Masuo Yasui, decided to walk the streets of Portland, Oregon, at night deliberately disobeying the curfew order. After failing to get a policeman to arrest him, he turned himself in at a police station so that he could contest DeWitt's authority in court. Yasui was soon joined by Gordon Hirabayashi, a twenty-four-year-old University of Washington student, who went to an FBI office to report his refusal to comply with removal orders. The third Japanese American to wage a legal challenge did not initially plan to be a protester. Fred Korematsu had simply wanted to remain in Oakland and San Francisco to be with his Italian American fiancée. But after he was discovered and arrested for violating the Army's exclusion order, Korematsu also decided to battle the government in court. Yasui, Hirabayashi, and Korematsu forced the Supreme Court to consider the constitutionality of the government's curfew and exclusion policies. When the Court affirmed the legality of the "mass evacuation," it established a legal precedent for the wartime removal of a single ethnic group that has never been officially overturned. Only in the case of Mitsuye Endo did the justices acknowledge a limitation to the government's powers

WESTERN DEFENSE COMMAND AND FOURTH ARMY
WARTIME CIVIL CONTROL ADMINISTRATION

Presidio of San Francisco, California
April 24, 1942

INSTRUCTIONS
TO ALL PERSONS OF
JAPANESE
ANCESTRY

Living in the Following Area:

All of those portions of the Counties of Contra Costa and Alameda, State of California, within the boundary beginning at Carquinez Strait; thence southerly on U. S. Highway No. 40 to its intersection with California State Highway No. 4, at or near Hercules; thence easterly on said Highway No. 4 to its intersection with California State Highway No. 21; thence southerly on said Highway No. 21 to its intersection with California State Highway No. 24, at Walnut Creek; thence westerly on said Highway No. 24 to the southerly limits of the City of Berkeley; thence following the said southerly city limits to San Francisco Bay; thence northerly and following the shore line of San Francisco Bay, through San Pablo Strait, and San Pablo Bay, to the point of beginning.

Pursuant to the provisions of Civilian Exclusion Order No. 19, this Headquarters, dated April 24, 1942, all persons of Japanese ancestry, both alien and non-alien, will be evacuated from the above area by 12 o'clock noon, P. W. T., Friday, May 1, 1942.

No Japanese person living in the above area will be permitted to change residence after 12 o'clock noon, P. W. T., Friday, April 24, 1942, without obtaining special permission from the representative of the Commanding General, Northern California Sector, at the Civil Control Station located at:

2345 Channing Way, Berkeley, California.

Such permits will only be granted for the purpose of uniting members of a family, or in cases of grave emergency.

The Civil Control Station is equipped to assist the Japanese population affected by this evacuation in the following ways:

1. Give advice and instructions on the evacuation.

2. Provide services with respect to the management, leasing, sale, storage or other disposition of most kinds of property, such as real estate, business and professional equipment, household goods, automobiles and livestock.

3. Provide temporary residence elsewhere for all Japanese in family groups.

4. Transport persons and a limited amount of clothing and equipment to their new residence.

The Following Instructions Must Be Observed:

1. A responsible member of each family, preferably the head of the family, or the person in whose name most of the property is held, and each individual living alone, will report to the Civil Control Station to receive further instructions. This must be done between 8:00 A. M. and 5:00 P. M. on Saturday, April 25, 1942, or between 8:00 A. M. and 5:00 P. M. on Sunday, April 26, 1942.

2. Evacuees must carry with them on departure for the Assembly Center, the following property:

(a) Bedding and linens (no mattress) for each member of the family;
(b) Toilet articles for each member of the family;
(c) Extra clothing for each member of the family;
(d) Sufficient knives, forks, spoons, plates, bowls and cups for each member of the family;
(e) Essential personal effects for each member of the family.

All items carried will be securely packaged, tied and plainly marked with the name of the owner and numbered in accordance with instructions obtained at the Civil Control Station.

The size and number of packages is limited to that which can be carried by the individual or family group.

3. No pets of any kind will be permitted.

4. The United States Government through its agencies will provide for the storage at the sole risk of the owner of the more substantial household items, such as iceboxes, washing machines, pianos and other heavy furniture. Cooking utensils and other small items will be accepted for storage if crated, packed and plainly marked with the name and address of the owner. Only one name and address will be used by a given family.

5. Each family, and individual living alone, will be furnished transportation to the Assembly Center or will be authorized to travel by private automobile in a supervised group. All instructions pertaining to the movement will be obtained at the Civil Control Station.

**Go to the Civil Control Station between the hours of 8:00 A. M. and 5:00 P. M.,
Saturday, April 25, 1942, or between the hours of 8:00 A. M. and 5:00 P. M.,
Sunday, April 26, 1942, to receive further instructions.**

J. L. DeWITT
Lieutenant General, U. S. Army
Commanding

SEE CIVILIAN EXCLUSION ORDER NO. 19.

This "evacuation" poster uses government euphemisms for the forcible removal of Japanese Americans. Courtesy Civil Liberties Public Education Fund.

to detain Japanese Americans. On December 18, 1944, the Supreme Court ruled in the Endo case that camp administrators had "no authority to subject citizens who are concededly loyal to its leave restrictions" and made it possible for at least some Japanese Americans to return to the West Coast.

Although a few individuals went to court to fight the removal and detention orders, most Japanese Americans complied with DeWitt's instructions. Few had any idea of their destinations when they were labeled, like luggage, with numbered identification tags at designated departure points in April and early May 1942. Most of the "assembly centers" were located at racetracks and fairgrounds, and many families stayed in hastily converted horse stalls that reeked of manure. Then, at the end of May, they were sent to camps run by the WRA, where barbed wire, watchtowers, and military police reminded them that they were prisoners who could not leave without the administrators' approval. Even those who received permission to leave the camps could not return to the West Coast until the exclusion order was lifted in December 1944.

Most internment camps were located on desert or swamp-like terrain. In some camps, winter temperatures dropped to 35 degrees below zero, and summer temperatures soared as high as 115 degrees. The hot and humid summers in the Arkansas camps bred swarms of chiggers and mosquitoes. The assistant project director at Minidoka, a camp in Idaho, described the camp as "hot, dusty, [and] desolate" and remarked on the "flat land, nothing growing but sagebrush, not a tree in sight." A WRA official noted a common problem in many camps: "a dust storm nearly every day for the first two months. . . . Fine, choking dust . . . swirled over the center. Traffic was sometimes forced to a standstill because there was no visibility."

Facilities differed from camp to camp, but all were spartan. Internees were assigned to a block consisting of fourteen barracks subdivided into four or six rooms. The average room for a family of six measured twenty by twenty-five feet. Privacy within the barracks proved elusive because room dividers often stopped short of the roof. Many internees, especially older women, were mortified by the lack of partitions in the communal bathrooms. Families constantly battled the dust that seeped through the barracks planks. The WRA supplied only canvas cots, a potbellied stove, and a lightbulb hanging from the ceiling. Resourceful internees later constructed makeshift furniture from scrap lumber and cultivated their own gardens to supplement the unfamiliar and unappetizing food served in the mess halls. Standing in line became an integral part of camp life. The WRA's assistant regional director once reported counting three hundred people waiting outside a mess hall.

At first, no internee could leave the center except for an emergency, and then only if chaperoned by someone not of Japanese ancestry. Regardless

A muddy quagmire in front of the barracks at Tule Lake, California. Courtesy National Archives, photo no. 210-G-B-134.

of education or training, Japanese American workers were subordinate to WRA personnel and received vastly lower wages of $12, $16, or $19 a month. For example, a WRA librarian might earn $167 a month, whereas her Japanese American staff members were paid only $16 for doing similar work. Moreover, wages and clothing allowances were often delayed, and the WRA failed to fulfill its promise to ship household goods to arriving internees. There were even rumors that WRA staff members at several camps stole food and other supplies.

WRA policies also exacerbated pre-existing tensions between Issei (first-generation) and Nisei (second-generation) community leaders. The government named Nisei leaders in the Japanese American Citizens League (JACL) as representatives of the entire ethnic community. Even though this middle-class, second-generation organization had fewer than eight thousand members before the war, government officials were pleased by JACL ultrapatriotic statements praising "American Democracy," vowing cooperation, and expressing gratitude for benevolent internment policies. Camp administrators accepted JACL advice to limit community government positions to citizens, to ban Japanese-language schools, and to prohibit the use of the Japanese language at public meetings. Whereas JACL leaders believed that cooperation, assimilation, and regaining the right to serve in the military were necessary to combat racism, many disgruntled internees, especially the disempowered Issei, derided JACL leaders as "inu" or dogs who collaborated with the government against the interests of the community.

As hostility toward the WRA grew, some internees vented their anger against JACL leaders suspected of being informers. The arrests of individuals accused of beating up suspected "inu" generated protests against the administration at the Poston and Manzanar Camps at the end of 1942. When the project director at Poston refused to release two men arrested for an attack, internees waged a general strike that shut down most camp services. Deciding to negotiate with the strikers, camp administrators agreed to release one suspect and to try the other within the camp rather than in an Arizona court. In return, strike leaders agreed to try to stop assaults against suspected "inu" and to promote harmony with the administration.

Similar protests at Manzanar, however, ended in bloodshed. The project director summoned the military police to put down a mass demonstration calling for the release of an arrested internee. When the crowd refused to disperse, military police sprayed tear gas, which was ineffective due to the wind. A member of the crowd started a car and aimed it at the police. While witnesses disagree about whether the police began firing before or after the car was started, all agree that they opened fire directly on the crowd, killing two people and wounding at least nine others. Even after the administration removed JACL leaders from the camp and moved suspected agitators to isolation camps (see map), tensions remained high.

Turmoil enveloped all of the camps in February 1943, when the WRA instituted a loyalty review program with little or no notice and without a clear explanation as to how the information gathered would be used. All internees over the age of seventeen were told to fill out a "leave clearance" application, which included ambiguously worded questions that confused many internees. Ironically, the WRA mistakenly assumed that the internees would be grateful for this expedited "leave clearance" program, which would allow them to move to the Midwest or East and volunteer for military service. JACL leaders had fought for the opportunity to serve in the armed forces and praised the War Department's decision to allow Japanese Americans to volunteer for a segregated combat unit on January 28, 1943. But many other internees resented being asked to shed blood for a country that had imprisoned them.

Unaware of the depth of internee fear and anger, WRA officials were shocked by the controversy generated by two of the questions on the leave application. Question 27 required internees to say whether they were "willing to serve in the armed forces of the United States on combat duty, wherever ordered." Question 28 asked, "Will you swear unqualified allegiance to the United States of America and faithfully defend the United States from any or all attack by foreign or domestic forces, and forswear any form of allegiance or obedience to the Japanese emperor, or any other foreign government, power or organization?" Taking for granted that both questions would be answered positively, the WRA didn't contemplate how foolish it was to ask elderly Issei to serve in combat. Some Nisei suspected that question 28 was designed to trap them into admitting an "allegiance" to the emperor they never had. The injustice of asking immigrants ineligible for American citizenship to become stateless by forswearing "any form of allegiance or obedience to the Japanese emperor" was recognized only belatedly. But even after WRA officials rephrased these questions, some internees still refused to complete the "leave clearance" forms to avoid being forced to resettle. After losing their businesses and property and being told that they could not return to the West Coast, some embittered internees were skeptical that they could start over in predominantly white communities in the Midwest and East.

Although about some 68,000 internees answered the two loyalty questions with an unqualified yes, approximately 5,300 answered "no no" and about 4,600 either refused to answer or qualified their responses. One WRA staff member noted how difficult it was to distinguish

> the No of protest against discrimination, the No of protest against a father interned apart from his family, the No of bitter antagonism to subordinations in the relocation center, the No of a gang sticking together, the No of thoughtless defiance, the No of family duty, the No of hopeless confusion, the No of fear of military service, and the No of felt loyalty to Japan.

Far from measuring "loyalty" to the United States or Japan, the questionnaire, another staff member noted, "sorted people chiefly into the disillusioned and the defiant as against the compliant and the hopeful."

Some of "the compliant and the hopeful" followed WRA procedures to leave camp for military service, jobs, or college programs. But of the almost 20,000 men in the camps who were eligible for military service, only 1,200 actually volunteered from behind barbed wire. Later, at the beginning of 1944, the Selective Service began drafting Japanese Americans. More than 300 men refused to comply with the draft while they and their families were still incarcerated. Many of these draft resisters served prison terms of two to four years, but they were pardoned by President Harry Truman in 1947. Other Japanese Americans agreed to offer "proof in blood" of their loyalty to the United States. Ultimately, approximately 23,000 Nisei, more than half from Hawaii, served in the 100th Infantry Battalion, the 442nd Regimental Combat Team, and the Military Intelligence Service during World War II. Fighting seven major campaigns in Italy and France, the 442nd suffered almost 9,500 casualties (300 percent of its original complement) and became the most decorated unit in American military history for its size and length of service. Japanese American servicemen acquired more than 18,000 individual decorations, 3,600 Purple Hearts, 350 Silver Stars, and 47 Distinguished Service Crosses. When President Truman presented the 100/442nd Regimental Combat Team with an eighth Presidential Distinguished Unit Citation in 1946, he proclaimed, "You fought not only the enemy, but you fought prejudice — and you won."

Other Japanese Americans left the camps through the WRA's "seasonal leave" program, developed in the summer of 1942 to address a shortage of farmworkers. In 1942 and 1943, more than eight thousand internees obtained work release furloughs. The WRA encouraged internees who passed the "loyalty test" to resettle in the interior states after February 1943. By December 1943, the National Japanese American Student Relocation Council was able to place more than two thousand Nisei in colleges in the Midwest and East. Then, on December 17, 1944, officials announced the termination of mass exclusion one day before the Supreme Court declared in the Endo case that the United States could no longer detain loyal citizens against their will. Once allowed to go back home, more than two-thirds of the internee population chose to return to the West Coast.

A significant number of "the disillusioned and the defiant," however, remained in camps even after the war ended in August 1945. The Tule Lake camp in northern California, which had been transformed into a "segregation center" for "disloyals," did not close until March 1946. Approximately one-third of the eighteen thousand residents at Tule Lake were people the WRA deemed "disloyal"; another third were members of their families; and the final third were "Old Tuleans," who, when the camp was designated as a segregation center in 1943, chose to remain with the "disloyals" rather than be forced to move a second time. The combination of this diverse internee population and a repressive administration created an explosive atmosphere at the segregation center. On November 4, 1943, the Army was called in to quell a demonstration, took over the camp, and declared martial law, which remained in effect until January 15, 1944. In the last half of 1944, the WRA allowed "resegregationists," who demanded a separation of those wanting to leave the United States for Japan and those at Tule Lake for other reasons, to dominate the camp. Using rumors, beatings, and in one case murder, the resegregationists intimidated inmates considered "fence-

President Truman's eighth Presidential Distinguished Unit Citation to the 100/442nd. Courtesy National Japanese American Historical Society.

sitters" or "loyal" to the United States. By the time the WRA brought the camp back under control, seven of every ten adult Nisei had renounced their citizenship.

The Department of Justice received more than 6,000 applications for renunciation of citizenship and approved 5,589 of them. This number represented 12.5 percent of the 70,000 citizens interned during the war. But even before many of these applications were processed, most of the "renunciants" tried to withdraw their requests. In fact, 5,409 citizens attempted to rescind their applications but the government ignored these attempts and proceeded with plans to deport these people to Japan. In August and September 1945, the renunciants who wanted to fight for their citizenship rights organized the Tule Lake Defense Committee and hired attorney Wayne M. Collins to represent them. Collins resisted pressure from the national American Civil Liberties Union to withdraw from the case and spent more than a

Guard tower at the Tule Lake Segregation Center. Courtesy National Archives, photo no. 210-CL-D-650-38.

decade fighting on behalf of the renunciants. In his suit, Collins argued that the Nisei had been coerced into renouncing their citizenship. He said that the government's forced removal and incarceration of Japanese Americans had subjected internees to "inhuman" treatment and extreme duress. To compound this injustice, the government had known about but had done nothing to restrain a small group of Japanese Americans at Tule Lake who terrorized many of the Nisei until they renounced their citizenship. Finally, after fourteen years, citizenship rights were restored to 4,978 Nisei.

Perhaps the most tragic example of "defiance" against the authorities was opposition to the closing of the camps. Instead of celebrating the prospect of freedom, many demoralized internees demanded that the government continue to provide for them or at least increase the amount of assistance given to resettlers. Many were afraid to leave the camps after hearing reports of how Japanese Americans outside of camp were subjected to arson, vandalism, and even gunfire. Many Issei men in their sixties didn't relish the prospect of starting over and felt that they were "entitled to receive com-

Tule Lake residents depart for Japan. Courtesy National Archives, photo no. 210-CL-R-15.

pensation from the Government for the losses which they experienced at the time of evacuation." Rejecting these calls for substantive redress, the WRA gave recalcitrant internees $25 and put them on trains back to their hometowns.

Churches and charity organizations helped "resettlers" find food and shelter, but many Issei men could find jobs only as janitors and gardeners. They had to rely on the income of their wives who worked in factories or as domestic servants. Their children, no longer barred from white-collar and professional jobs, were able to participate in the postwar economic boom. But even many "successful" Nisei bore psychological scars from the incarceration. Community activist Amy Ishii has compared internees' feelings of guilt and shame with the self-blame experienced by some rape victims. Many tried to repress memories of the camps because, as former internee Ben Takeshita later testified before a government commission in 1981, they couldn't bear remembering how internment had divided friends and family members:

> The resulting in-fighting, beatings, and verbal abuses left families torn apart, parents against children, brothers against sisters, relatives against relatives, and friends against friends. So bitter was all this that even to this day, there are many amongst us who do not speak about that period for fear that the same harsh feelings might rise up again to the surface.

Other Japanese Americans, former internee Mary Oda explained to the same commission, didn't talk about the camps to spare their children "the burden of shame and feelings of rejection by their fellow Americans."

Historians and Internment: From Relocation Centers to Concentration Camps

In the immediate postwar period, only a few Japanese American accounts of camp life, such as Mine Okubo's *Citizen 13660* (1946) and Monica Sone's *Nisei Daughter* (1953), were published. Most former internees were far too busy trying to rebuild their lives to prepare "histories" of internment. Hoping to forget the incarceration, few wrote or even read works on internment before the 1970s. Consequently, most of the histories of internment published in the two decades that followed the war were written by WRA officials and academics who had conducted research on Japanese Americans in the camps. These works paint a very different picture of the causes and consequences of internment from the one presented by studies in the 1970s. Why did the scholarship change? The studies produced in the 1970s were written by scholars influenced by the civil rights movement, protests against the Vietnam War, and the demonstrations of ethnic and racial pride that spread throughout the 1960s and 1970s. These social movements generated a different set of assumptions about the nature of government, politics, protest, and ethnic culture.

Most of the writers in the 1940s and 1950s believed that government officials might make mistakes but were generally well-intentioned. In their accounts, the decision to intern Japanese Americans is presented as a misguided policy that created hardships for those forced to leave their homes during the war. Camp administrators, according to these writers, tried to help Japanese Americans adjust to life in the camps, prove their patriotism, and assimilate into "mainstream America." Although these writers don't always agree on the extent of the success of these policies, most laud the motives and goals of camp officials. Most of their accounts praise Japanese American forbearance and cooperation with the government and lament the outbreak of protests within the camps. Even writers who express sympathy for Japanese American resisters portray such protests as unfortunate and futile.

By contrast, researchers in the 1970s had a different interpretation of why Japanese Americans were interned and how they responded to their incarceration. The view of internment presented in their accounts emphasizes a long history of government oppression against people of color. Many of these scholars argue that internment was not just a product of the war or the anti-Japanese movement on the West Coast. Instead, internment was part of a pattern of systematic government discrimination against racial groups in America. Distrusting official explanations of internment, these writers scrutinized private as well as public statements to provide a more detailed indictment of the motives of the architects of the policy. They also criticize publications from the 1940s and 1950s for perpetuating government euphemisms such as "evacuation," "assembly centers," and "relocation centers." Many insist that Japanese Americans were imprisoned in "concentration camps" during the war. They denounce camp administrators for repressing protests within the camps and promoting the assimilation of Japanese Americans. The heroes in most of these accounts are not Japanese Americans who cooperated with officials but internees who resisted the incarceration, defied camp policies, and proclaimed pride in their Japanese heritage.

These later accounts bear little resemblance to those provided by camp administrators in the 1940s. As one might expect, accounts written by officials who managed the camps are self-serving. Although they generally criticize the anti-Japanese sentiment that led to the mass removal of Japanese Americans, they invariably portrayed the camps in a positive light. In accounts such as *WRA: A Story of Human Conservation* (1946), administrators are portrayed as compassionate defenders of internees against the racists who put them in the camps and accused the WRA of "coddling" internees. The camps, such accounts claim, provided "refuge from the storms of racial prejudice and the disruptions of total war," and the WRA dispersion policies gave the Nisei "new opportunities" and "confidence in themselves."

Publications by sociologists and anthropologists employed by the WRA as "community analysts" during the war are not so effusive. The twenty-seven white social scientists whom camp officials hired to interpret and help manage the internee population did not minimize the internees' financial and emotional problems. *The Governing of Men: General Principles and Recommendations Based on Experience at a Japanese Relocation Camp* by Alexander Leighton (1945) and *Impounded People: Japanese Americans in the Relocation Centers* by Edward Spicer and others (1946) describe the harsh conditions at the camps, the internees' feelings of alienation and frustration, and the devastation wrought by the loyalty questionnaire. Yet even as these works recount a history of strikes, riots, and mass demonstrations, they present resistance as an unfortunate product of miscommunication and misunderstanding rather than a legitimate response to incarceration. Like many Americans at the time, most of these researchers took it for granted that protests were wrong and that the social scientists' role in helping control the internees was ethical. In fact, *The Governing of Men* includes a manual on managing future camps and proclaims that "communities under stress" are "ripe for change." Manzanar analyst Morris E. Opler wrote a brief for Fred Korematsu challenging the constitutionality of internment, and Tule Lake analyst Marvin K. Opler prepared a brief denouncing the unfairness of the segregation and renunciation process. Neither analyst, however, allowed his name to be printed on the brief or published any articles or books expressing his outrage at the injustice of incarceration.

Publications by the Japanese American Evacuation and Resettlement Study (JERS) are more critical of camp administrators. Under the supervision of Dorothy Thomas, a professor at the University of California, the JERS conducted field research within the camps throughout the war. Not responsible for the removal or control of Japanese Americans, the three white researchers, twelve Japanese American field-workers, and at least twelve other internees who assisted JERS research were directed simply to record events as they happened. But as Yuji Ichioka notes in *Views from Within: The Japanese American Evacuation and Resettlement Study* (1989), the assumptions and methodology of these researchers were controversial. In exchange for cooperation from the federal government, the social scientists agreed not to publish or publicly describe their findings until after the war. Thomas also compromised JERS independence by agreeing to submit monthly reports to camp administrators.

The JERS researchers could not be "detached" observers of something as wrenching as internment. Internee field-workers not only suffered the trauma of incarceration but also risked community ostracism and even violence because of the suspicion that they were FBI or WRA informants. Richard Nishimoto, the internee Thomas relied on most to help her understand the camp experience and the coauthor of *The Spoilage* (1946), concealed his JERS affiliation and actively influenced the politics at Poston. Although *The Spoilage* provides an early indictment of the WRA's discriminatory policies and incompetent supervision of militant resegregationists at Tule Lake, the study also raises several ethical questions. The book's supposedly "impartial" description of events at Tule Lake was based on field notes by Rosalie Wax (née Hankey), who later admitted, in *Doing Fieldwork: Warnings and Advice* (1971), to having deceived administrators and internees, befriended certain factional leaders, become a "fanatic" who exulted in the murder of an "accommodator," and informed on two internees to the Justice Department. Tule Lake internee Kazue Matsuda also accused Hankey of violating a promise of confidentiality, supplying false information about Matsuda's activities to the Justice Department, and ultimately causing her to be separated from her children. Ironically, despite Hankey's admiration for some Tule Lake dissident leaders, authors Thomas and Nishimoto chose the title *The Spoilage,* which further stigmatized those internees the government had pronounced "disloyal."

The second JERS study, Thomas's *The Salvage* (1952), includes fifteen life histories of Nisei resettlers interviewed by Charles Kikuchi and gave Japa-

nese Americans a chance to describe the impact of internment on their as-
pirations, occupational mobility, and family relations. Though quite informative, Kikuchi's interviewees were all urban, college-educated, Christian
or secular Nisei men and women. All criticized the decision to intern Japanese Americans, but many praised the benefits of postwar dispersion and assimilation. Yet one can't help but wonder whether they were truly "salvaged"
when so many expressed anxiety at an association with anything "Japanese,"
feared talking about the camps to white Americans, and tried to suppress
memories of the camps.

The final JERS study, *Prejudice, War, and the Constitution* (1954), provides
an early critique of the decision to intern Japanese Americans. It documents
that internment was not the product of "military necessity" and questions
the Supreme Court decisions affirming the constitutionality of internment.
Although it holds President Roosevelt, the War Department, and the courts
"responsible" for this injustice, the only advocate of internment examined
in great detail is General DeWitt. The book's dispassionate tone may reflect
the fact that it was commissioned by Thomas to counter the "unscholarly"
judgments in Morton Grodzins's *Americans Betrayed: Politics and the Japanese
Evacuation* (1949). Grodzins had been a JERS research assistant, and his dissertation censured the racism of West Coast politicians, journalists, and economic interest groups who advocated internment. Dismayed by Grodzins's
"propaganda," Thomas and a University of California investigative subcom-
mittee urged the University of Chicago to reject his manuscript. University
of Chicago Press director William Terry Couch decided to publish the book
anyway and compared suppression of Grodzins's research to concealing
"information concerning white treatment of the Negro from the public at
large." University of California officials, fearful of appearing to censor scholarship for political reasons, backed down, and the book was published, but
Couch was fired for antagonizing another university.

During the 1970s, a new generation of scholars embraced controversial
interpretations and provided very different perspectives on the history of
internment. These post-JERS researchers promoted "revisionist" histories
that challenged earlier depictions of the causes and consequences of internment. Their studies questioned the way publications in the 1940s and
1950s emphasized a history of wartime hysteria, heroic volunteer soldiers,
and beneficial assimilation. Instead, they highlighted the racism that led to
the mass incarceration, the suffering and resistance within the camps, and
a postwar legacy of pain and silence.

The writings in this book reflect the impact of revisionist scholarship.
The first selection, an excerpt from Roger Daniels's *Concentration Camps
USA* (1971), condemns the way military and government officials fabricated
a "military necessity" rationale for internment. A pioneering revisionist
scholar, Daniels has always insisted that Japanese Americans were confined

in "concentration camps." He has repeatedly reminded readers that both President Roosevelt and Chief Justice Owen Roberts used the term "concentration camp" when talking about Japanese Americans. Daniels acknowledges that the American camp experience was very different from the Nazi Holocaust and that more Japanese Americans were born in camps than died there. Nevertheless, Daniels insists that there were important parallels. Both American and German camps confined individuals simply on the basis of ancestry, without charge or trial. Both established barbed-wire compounds and military patrols. And although Japanese Americans were never subjected to systematic execution, several inmates were shot and killed by armed guards.

Other revisionist scholars have attacked WRA policies. Richard Drinnon's *Keeper of Concentration Camps: Dillon S. Myer and American Racism* (1987) denounces the head of the WRA and the Bureau of Indian Affairs as a paternalistic, self-styled "Great White Father" bent on destroying native cultures and exemplifying the "banality of evil." JACL leaders who cooperated with the government also have come under critical scrutiny by scholars challenging JACL hagiographic accounts such as *Nisei: The Quiet Americans* (1969), *JACL: In Quest of Justice* (1982), and *They Call Me Moses Masaoka* (1987). Articles by Yuji Ichioka, Bob Kumamoto, and Paul Spickard contain evidence that JACL leaders informed on immigrant leaders to the FBI, proposed the creation of a "suicide battalion" of volunteer soldiers, and urged the WRA to limit Issei influence in the camps.

Revisionist scholars also have questioned earlier depictions of camp protests as sporadic incidents caused by misconceptions and small groups of agitators. In *Amerasia Journal*, a product of the Asian American movement, Gary Y. Okihiro, Arthur A. Hansen, and David A. Hacker have presented a history of widespread and continuous resistance within the camps. Okihiro's "Japanese Resistance in America's Concentration Camps: A Re-evaluation" (1973) proposes that "the assumptions of the revisionist histories of slave and colonized groups provide a more realistic basis for an analysis of Japanese reaction to concentration camp authority than do the older notions of Japanese 'loyalty' and helplessness." Moreover, Okihiro redefined protest to include not only organized demonstrations but also work slowdowns and the proliferation of Japanese cultural societies in the camps. Hansen and Hacker's "The Manzanar Riot: An Ethnic Perspective" (1974) extends this analysis of cultural resistance to WRA Americanization campaigns and interprets the "riot" as evidence of the internees' struggle for self-determination, the persistence of ethnic identity, and group solidarity.

Until the 1980s, revisionist scholars had to reinterpret WRA, JERS, and court records because few Japanese Americans were willing to provide oral histories of internment. The redress movement of the 1970s and 1980s exhumed former internees' buried memories of the camps. At first, the idea of redress had little support within the Japanese American community. In 1970, former internee Edison Uno persuaded the JACL to pass a resolution calling for legislation to make amends for "the worst mistakes of World War II," but the organization hesitated to take more concrete action. Grassroots activists within the JACL and other community organizations began mounting pilgrimages to former camp sites and "day of remembrance" programs to encourage former internees to share their personal histories of internment. They urged Japanese Americans to read revisionist writing, such as Michi Weglyn's *Years of Infamy* (1976). These activists also established historical landmarks at former camp sites; convinced the government to repeal Title II of the 1950 Internal Security Act, which authorized the government to maintain detention camps for suspected "saboteurs"; and successfully lobbied the U.S. government to officially revoke Executive Order 9066.

By the beginning of the 1980s, these experienced activists could mobilize significant community support for redress. Activists within the JACL successfully lobbied the government to establish the Commission on Wartime Relocation and Internment of Civilians, which held hearings on the causes and consequences of internment. These hearings, held throughout the country in 1981, encouraged Japanese Americans to share their pain and anger at the injustice of internment. More than five hundred Japanese Americans testified at the hearings. These cathartic accounts of anguish experienced during the war intensified and deepened the community's commitment to redress. After the commission called on the government to provide a formal apology and monetary compensation, Japanese Americans submitted and lobbied for redress legislation. In 1988, this effort was rewarded by the passage of the Civil Liberties Act of 1988, which provided an official apology and a payment of $20,000 to each surviving internee.

Well before the first checks were issued in 1990, the redress movement had promoted a new understanding of the history of internment by helping to unleash a flood of oral histories, memoirs, poetry, fiction, and documentaries by former internees and their children. Valerie Matsumoto's *Farming the Home Place* (1993) manifests the impact of these new oral history sources. Matsumoto's interviews helped her recover the diverse experiences of Japanese Americans from one of the few communities to retain land and property during the war. No longer relegated to being victims, patriots, or resisters, the men and women who appear in the book express a variety of feelings experienced before, during, and after the war.

Matsumoto is only one of many recent scholars who have broadened our view of internment by exploring previously neglected groups. Research by Mei Nakano, Dana Takagi, Evelyn Nakano Glenn, and Sylvia Junko Yanagisako has recognized the importance of women and gender as a category of analysis. Scholars have learned more about the Department of Justice camps thanks to John Christgau's study of "alien internees" and C. Harvey

Gardiner's research on U.S. policies toward Peruvian internees. Paul Spickard has drawn attention to the hardships of Amerasian children and non-Japanese spouses in the camps, Thomas James has examined educational policies, and Gary Okihiro has given voice to internees from Hawaii in *Cane Fires* (1991). The anthology *Japanese Americans: From Relocation to Redress* (1986) provides multiple perspectives on life before, during, and after internment. Finally, now that historians no longer feel compelled to emphasize Japanese American "loyalty" to justify redress, scholars such as Yuji Ichioka, John Stephan, and Brian Masaru Hayashi have begun to explore the pro-Japanese nationalist sentiment of some Japanese Americans and the experiences of a few who lived in Japan and worked for the Japanese government or served in the Japanese military during the war.

PART TWO

Some Current Questions

The selections that follow deal with some of the issues about the internment of Japanese Americans that now interest historians. Other questions and other selections could have been chosen, but these show the current state of the conversation. Each selection is preceded by a headnote that introduces both its specific subject and its author. After the headnote come Questions for a Closer Reading. The headnote and the questions offer signposts that will allow you to understand more readily what the author is saying. The selections are uncut and they include the original notes. The notes are also signposts for further exploration. If an issue that the author raises intrigues you, use the notes to follow it up. At the end of all the selections are more questions, under the heading Making Connections. Turn to these after you have read the selections, and use them to bring the whole discussion together. In order to answer them, you may find that you need to reread. But no historical source yields up all that is within it to a person content to read it just once.

1. Why were Japanese Americans interned during World War II?

Roger Daniels

The Decision for Mass Evacuation

Six days after Roger Daniels's fourteenth birthday, the Japanese attacked Pearl Harbor. Like most Americans, Daniels wanted to be part of a "unified national effort" to defend the country, so he misrepresented his age in 1944 and joined the merchant marine. After the war, experiences in the labor and civil rights movement led Daniels to question the "culture of consensus" that developed in the 1950s. He worked for the Congress of Industrial Organizations and the International Longshoremen's and Warehousemen's Union before becoming an undergraduate at the University of Houston. In Houston, he tried to foster exchanges between white students at his school and African American students at Texas Southern University. By the time Daniels entered the graduate history program at the University of California at Los Angeles, he knew he wanted to conduct a study on racism. His dissertation, *The Politics of Prejudice: The Anti-Japanese Movement in California and the Struggle for Japanese Exclusion,* was published in 1962. In the preface, Daniels explains his "ulterior motive" in researching campaigns to end Japanese immigration by labor unions, progressives, and other "groups supposedly dedicated to democracy": "I am persuaded that not nearly enough attention has been paid to the antidemocratic threads that make up a goodly part of the fabric of our national heritage, and that by careful studies of these threads we may discover hitherto unnoticed patterns."

Even before he finished *The Politics of Prejudice,* Daniels had decided to explore the "antidemocratic threads" that caused internment. In fact, he would later say that if more government material had been declassified, he would have published *Concentration Camps USA: Japanese Americans and World War II* (1971) as his first rather than his second book. In this period before the Freedom of Information Act of 1976, many government records were restricted. While examining Department of Justice sources, Daniels learned that he was supposed to alert archivists about any FBI documents he came across so that they could be removed from the files. But he worked out an arrangement with a helpful archivist who allowed him to view a file and then go to the bathroom (where he took notes from memory on the material) before handing it back. These notes helped him find other corroborating evidence that he could then quote. The biggest boon to Daniels's research was the assistance offered by Dr. Stetson Conn, former chief military historian of the U.S. Army. In the summer of 1969, Conn gave Daniels access to his personal notes on many items no longer available at the National Archives. Conn even underlined his notes on the phone conversations between the architects of internment that Daniels would later cite as key evidence in his condemnation of the decision.

After examining these phone conversations, memos, letters, and other sources, Daniels argued in *Concentration Camps USA* that internment was not just a "wartime mistake" but reflected "one of the central themes of American history — the theme of white supremacy, of American racism." This selection analyzes the impact of racial attitudes on officials as they considered a variety of proposals for dealing with Japanese Americans. In "The Decision for Mass Evacuation," Daniels recounts how civilians who controlled the Army developed plans to remove Japanese Americans from the West Coast. Although some politicians, journalists, and nativist groups demanded the removal of all "Japs" from the West Coast, other officials, especially within the Justice Department, expressed concern about disregarding the rights of citizens. Official military reports also discounted the need for mass removal. Even Lieutenant General John L. DeWitt vacillated in his views of internment. As Daniels notes, Major General Allen W. Gullion and his subordinate Karl Bendetsen repeatedly lobbied DeWitt and members of the War Department to support mass removal and incarceration. Other proposals, such as creating "Jap-free" zones around security installations or allowing voluntary resettlement to the central valleys of California, were considered. But ultimately, as Daniels's pioneering research demonstrates, Gullion and Bendetsen succeeded in winning over Assistant Secretary of War John McCloy and Secretary of War Henry Stimson at the beginning of February 1942. Accepting their advice, President Franklin Delano Roosevelt signed Executive Order 9066 and gave DeWitt the authority to remove and intern Japanese Americans.

The evidence Daniels uncovered played a major role in winning redress for former internees. Even before he published *Concentration Camps USA*, Daniels was active in the Japanese American community. In 1967, he was a co-organizer of the first academic conference on the causes and consequences of internment. He appeared before the U.S. Senate in 1980 to affirm that "scholarly opinion has condemned the relocation" and to call for the creation of a commission to "serve an educational purpose by reminding Americans about one of the wrongs of our past."[1]

Once the Commission on Wartime Relocation and Internment of Civilians was established, Daniels became a consultant, briefed the commissioners, wrote several memorandums, and answered staff questions. He declared monetary redress "entirely appropriate" in an introduction he wrote for a position paper submitted by the Japanese American Citizens League to the commission. Because of his expertise, the commission asked him to read and comment on the draft version of the historical text of its report. In 1982, this landmark report concluded that internment had been caused not by military necessity but by "race prejudice, war hysteria, and a failure of political leadership."[2]

Daniels, a professor of history at the University of Cincinnati since 1976, persuaded a Republican congressman from his home state to support redress legislation. An eminent scholar in Asian American and immigration history, he has written numerous books and articles, including *Asian America: Chinese and Japanese in the United States since 1850* (1988), *Prisoners without Trial: Japanese Americans and World War II* (1993), and *Coming to America: Immigration and Ethnicity in American Life* (1990). He also has served as a consultant for several documentary films and historical exhibits and has been president of the Immigration History Society and the Society for Historians of the Gilded Age and the Progressive Era.

Questions for a Closer Reading

1. According to Daniels, who were the real architects of internment? What were their motives and strategies for winning support for mass removal and incarceration?

2. Compare the assessments of Japanese Americans by advocates and opponents of mass exclusion and internment. What views had the most influence on policy decisions?

3. What alternatives to internment were proposed? Why was there such a stark difference between the treatment of people of Japanese ancestry in Hawaii and the treatment of those on the West Coast?

4. Does Daniels's research effectively contradict claims by government officials that internment was required by "military necessity"?

5. Daniels provides a much harsher view of government policies and racial attitudes than earlier scholars. Based on the research presented in this selection, would you agree with Daniels's conclusion that Japanese Americans were imprisoned in "concentration camps"?

Notes

1. Commission on Wartime Relocation and Internment of Civilians Act, Hearing before the Committee on Governmental Affairs, United States Senate, 96th Congress, Second Session on S. 1647, March 18, 1980 (Washington, D.C.: U.S. Government Printing Office, 1980), 16–17.

2. Commission on Wartime Relocation and Internment of Civilians, *Personal Justice Denied: Report of the Commission on Wartime Relocation and Internment of Civilians* (Washington, D.C.: U.S. Government Printing Office, 1982), 18.

The Decision for Mass Evacuation

December 1941 was a month of calamities which saw West Coast opinion harden against the Japanese; during January, as the war news got worse and worse and it became apparent that the Japanese audacity at Pearl Harbor would not be quickly avenged, the national climate of opinion, and Congressional opinion in particular, began to veer toward the West Coast view. That this climate had to be created is shown by an examination of the *Congressional Record*. Not only was there no concerted strong feeling exhibited against the Japanese Americans, but in the first weeks after Pearl Harbor members of the California delegation defended them publicly. (The only trace of hostility shown by a California solon in early December was a telephone call that the junior senator, Democrat Sheridan Downey, made to the Army on the night of December 7 suggesting that DeWitt prompt Governor Olson to declare some sort of curfew on "Japs.") On December 10, for example, Bertrand W. Gearhart, a four-term Republican congressman from Fresno and an officer of the American Legion, read a telegram professing loyalty to the United States from an Issei leader in his district whom Gearhart described as an "American patriot." Five days later, when John Rankin (D-Miss.), the leading nativist in the lower house, called for "deporting every Jap who claims, or has claimed, Japanese citizenship, or sympathizes with Japan in this war," he was answered by another Californian, Leland M. Ford, a Santa Monica Republican:

> These people are American-born. They cannot be deported . . . whether we like it or whether we do not. This is their country. . . . [When] they join the armed forces . . . they must take this oath of allegiance . . . and I see no particular reason at this particular time why they should not. I believe that every one of these people should make a clear, clean acknowledgement.[1]

Roger Daniels, "The Decision for Mass Evacuation," *Concentration Camps USA: Japanese Americans and World War II* (New York: Holt, Rinehart & Winston, 1971), 42–73.

Despite the lack of Congressional concern, by the end of December momentum was gathering for more drastic action against the Japanese and against enemy aliens generally. On December 30 the Justice Department made the first of many concessions to the military, concessions that had little to do either with due process or the realities of the situation. On that date Attorney General Biddle informed the Provost Marshal General's office that he had authorized the issuance of search warrants for any house in which an enemy alien lived, merely on the representation that there was reasonable cause to believe that there was contraband on the premises. Contraband had already been defined to include anything that might be used as a weapon, any explosive (many Issei farmers used dynamite to clear stumps), radio transmitters, any radio that had a shortwave band, and all but the simplest cameras. For the next few months thousands of houses where Japanese lived were subjected to random search. Although much "contraband" was found (most of it in two Issei-owned sporting goods stores), the FBI itself later stipulated that none of it was sinister in nature and reported that there was no evidence at all that any of it was intended for subversive use. But the mere fact of these searches, widely reported in the press, added to the suspicion with which the Japanese were viewed. These searches, like so much of the anti-Japanese movement, were part of a self-fulfilling prophecy: one is suspicious of the Japanese, so one searches their houses; the mere fact of the search, when noticed ("the FBI went through those Jap houses on the other side of town"), creates more suspicion.

For individual Japanese families, these searches intensified the insecurity and terror they already felt. One fifteen-year-old girl in San Jose, California reported what must have been an all-too-routine occurrence:

One day I came home from school to find the two F.B.I. men at our front door. They asked permission to search the house. One man looked through the front rooms, while the other searched the back rooms. Trembling with fright, I followed and watched each of the men look around. The investigators examined the mattresses, and the dresser and looked under the beds. The gas range, piano, and sofa were thoroughly inspected. Since I was the only one at home, the F.B.I. questioned me, but did not procure sufficient evidence of Fifth Columnists in our family. This made me very happy, even if they did mess up the house.[2]

Concurrent with its more stringent search order, the Department of Justice and the Provost Marshal General's office decided to send representatives to DeWitt's headquarters in San Francisco; the two men sent — James Rowe, Jr., Assistant Attorney General and a former Presidential assistant, and Major (later Colonel) Karl R. Bendetsen, chief of the Aliens Division,

Provost Marshal General's office — were key and mutually antagonistic figures in the bureaucratic struggle over the fate of the West Coast Japanese. Rowe, during his short visit in California, exercised a moderating influence on the cautious General DeWitt, who often seemed to be the creature of the last strong personality with whom he had contact. Bendetsen represented a chief (Gullion) who wanted not only exclusion of the Japanese from the West Coast but also the transfer of supervisory authority over all enemy aliens in the United States from the civilian control of the Department of Justice to the military control of his office. Bendetsen soon became the voice of General DeWitt in matters concerning aliens, and was well rewarded for his efforts. A graduate of Stanford Law School, he had gone on to active duty as a captain in 1940, and in the process of evacuating the Japanese he would gain his colonel's eagles before he turned thirty-five. After Bendetsen's arrival, Gullion arranged with DeWitt that the West Coast commander go out of normal channels and deal directly with the Provost Marshal on matters concerning aliens. The result of this seemingly routine bureaucratic shuffle was highly significant; as Stetson Conn has pointed out, the consequence of this arrangement was that "the responsible Army command headquarters in Washington [that is, Chief of Staff George C. Marshall and his immediate staff] had little to do during January and February 1942 with the plans and decisions for Japanese evacuation."[3]

Telephone conversations and correspondence between DeWitt's headquarters and the Provost Marshal General's office in late December and early January reveal the tremendous pressures that the soldiers were putting on the civilians. According to General Gullion, the Justice Department's representatives, James Rowe, Jr., and Edward J. Ennis, were apologetic about the slowness of the Justice Department, an apparent criticism of their chief, the Attorney General. At about the same time Gullion was complaining that "the Attorney General is not functioning" and threatened to have Secretary Stimson complain to the President. DeWitt was, as usual, vacillating. Within the same week he told the Provost Marshal General's office that "it would be better if . . . this thing worked through the civil channels," but a few days later insisted that "I don't want to go after this thing piece meal. I want to do it on a mass basis, all at the same time."[4]

The arrival of Bendetsen at DeWitt's San Francisco headquarters seemed to strengthen the West Coast commander's resolve. Before Bendetsen left Washington he had drafted an Executive Order transferring authority over aliens to the War Department, but the Provost Marshal General's office felt that since the Justice Department's representatives were so apologetic, it "wasn't quite fair" to take over without giving them a chance to come up to the Army's standards. Shortly after his arrival in San Francisco, Bendetsen drafted a memo that quickly became the guideline for DeWitt's policy.

It called for an immediate and complete registration of all alien enemies, who were to be photographed and fingerprinted. These records were to be kept in duplicate, one set to be kept in the community in which the alien resided, the other in a central office. The purpose was to set up what Bendetsen called a "Pass and Permit System." Doubtful that the Attorney General would agree to this, Bendetsen's memo concluded with what had become the refrain of the Provost Marshal General's men: if Justice won't do it, the War Department must.

The next day, January 4, in a conference at his Presidio headquarters attended by Rowe, Bendetsen, and representatives of other federal departments and officials in local government, DeWitt made some of his position clear, stressing, as he always did to civilians, what he called the military necessity.

> We are at war and this area — eight states — has been designated as a theater of operations. I have approximately 240,000 men at my disposal. . . . [There are] approximately 288,000 enemy aliens . . . which we have to watch. . . . I have little confidence that the enemy aliens are law-abiding or loyal in any sense of the word. Some of them yes; many, no. Particularly the Japanese. I have no confidence in their loyalty whatsoever. I am speaking now of the native born Japanese — 117,000 — and 42,000 in California alone.[5]

One result of this conference was that the Department of Justice agreed to go further than it had previously: enemy aliens were to be re-registered under its auspices, the FBI would conduct large-scale "spot" raids, something DeWitt was particularly eager for, and, most significantly, a large number of restricted, or Category A, zones would be established around crucial military and defense installations on the Pacific Coast. Entry to these zones would be on a pass basis. Assistant Secretary of War John J. McCloy later described this program as "the best way to solve" the West Coast alien problem.

> . . . establish limited restricted areas around the airplane plants, the forts, and other important military installations . . . we might call these military reservations in substance and exclude everyone — whites, yellows, blacks, greens — from that area and then license back into the area those whom we felt there was no danger to be expected from . . . then we can cover the legal situation . . . in spite of the constitution. . . . You may, by that process, eliminate all the Japs [alien and citizen] but you might conceivably permit some to come back whom you are quite certain are free from any suspicion.[6]

In addition to the Category A zones, there were to be Category B zones, consisting of the rest of the coastal area, in which enemy aliens and citizen

Japanese would be allowed to live and work under rigidly prescribed conditions. Although DeWitt and the other Army people were constantly complaining about the slowness of the Justice Department, they quickly found that setting up these zones was easier said than done. DeWitt did not forward his first recommendations for Category A areas to the War Department until January 21, more than two weeks after the San Francisco conference.

On January 16 Representative Leland Ford, the Santa Monica Republican who had opposed stern treatment for the Japanese on the floor of the House in mid-December, had changed his mind. Ford had received a number of telegrams and letters from California suggesting removal of Japanese from vital coastal areas — the earliest seems to have been a January 6 telegram from Mexican American movie star Leo Carillo — and by mid-January had come around to their point of view. He urged Secretary of War Henry L. Stimson to have "all Japanese, whether citizens or not, . . . placed in inland concentration camps." Arguing that native-born Japanese either were or were not loyal to the United States, Ford developed a simple test for loyalty: any Japanese willing to go to a concentration camp was a patriot; therefore it followed that unwillingness to go was a proof of disloyalty to the United States. Stimson and his staff mulled over this letter for ten days, and then replied (in a letter drafted by Bendetsen, now back from the Pacific Coast) giving the congressman a certain amount of encouragement. "The internment of over a hundred thousand people," Stimson wrote, "involves many complex considerations." The basic responsibility, Stimson pointed out, putting the finger on his Cabinet colleague Francis Biddle, has been delegated to the Attorney General. Nevertheless, the Secretary continued, "the Army is prepared to provide internment facilities in the interior to the extent necessary." Assuring Ford that the Army was aware of the dangers on the Pacific Coast, Stimson informed him that the military were submitting suggestions to the Justice Department, and advised him to present his views to the Attorney General.[7]

The same day that Ford wrote Stimson, January 16, another federal department became involved in the fate of the West Coast Japanese. Agriculture Secretary Claude Wickard, chiefly concerned with increasing farm production — "Food Can Win the War" was his line — called a meeting in his office at which the War, Labor, Navy, Justice, and Treasury Departments were represented. He had become alarmed over investigative reports from his agents on the West Coast, who were concerned both about the fate of the Japanese and the threat to food production. Wickard had been informed that although violence against the Japanese farmers was an isolated phenomenon, greatly exaggerated by the press, nevertheless it was quite clear that the Japanese rural population was "terrified."

They do not leave their homes at night, and will not, even in the daytime, enter certain areas populated by Filipinos. The police authorities are probably not sympathetic to the Japanese and are giving them only the minimum protection. Investigation of actual attacks on Japanese have been merely perfunctory and no prosecutions have been initiated.[8]

The federal officials then concluded that the whole "propaganda campaign" against the Japanese was essentially a conspiracy designed to place Japanese-owned and -leased farm lands into white hands; the real aim was to "eliminate Japanese competition." Wickard's West Coast representatives urged him to take positive steps both to maintain agricultural production and to preserve and protect the property and persons of the Japanese farmers.

Wickard's action was not exactly along the lines recommended by the men in the field. He did urge immediate federal action "so that the supply of vegetables for the military forces and the civilian population will not be needlessly curtailed." But Wickard also felt that the fears and suspicions of the general public — particularly the West Coast public — should be taken into account. He seemed to envision a sort of large agricultural cultural reservation in the central valleys of California on which the Japanese could "carry on their normal farming operations" after being removed from "all strategic areas." In this way, Wickard felt, the country could protect itself from "possible subversive Japanese activities," provide "limited protection to all Japanese whose conduct is above suspicion," and at the same time "avoid incidents that might provide an excuse for cruel treatment for our people in Japanese occupied territory." As for the agricultural lands in the coastal area which the Japanese had tilled, Wickard suggested that Mexicans might be brought in to replace them.[9]

Also, by mid-January, the urban Japanese, if not terrorized as were their rural cousins, were feeling more and more hopeless and demoralized. An occasional militant like James Y. Sakamoto, a Japanese American Citizens League (JACL) official in Seattle, could indignantly protest against Representative Ford's evacuation proposal which went out on the Associated Press wire on January 21.

"This is our country," Sakamoto pointed out, "we were born and raised here . . . have made our homes here . . . [and] we are ready to give our lives, if necessary, to defend the United States." Ford's drastic measures, he insisted, were not in the best interests of the nation. But even a Nisei leader like Sakamoto felt compelled to admit that there was some kind of subversive danger from the older generation of Japanese. The Seattle Nisei, he stated, were "actively cooperating" with the authorities "to uncover all subversive activity in our midst" and, if necessary, he concluded, the Nisei were "ready to stand as protective custodians over our parent generation to guard against danger to the United States arising from their midst."[10] One of the standard complaints quite properly raised by Americans in denouncing totalitarian regimes is that their police states turn children against their parents; it is rarely remarked that, in this instance at least, such too was the function of American democracy.

But for those really in charge, the agonizing distinctions between father and son, between alien and citizen, were essentially irrelevant. By mid-January, perhaps as a way of answering the points made by Representative Ford, Chief of Staff George C. Marshall ordered the Provost Marshal General's office to prepare a memorandum on the West Coast Japanese situation. Bendetsen, the natural drafter for such a report, called General DeWitt to ask what his attitude would be if "the Department of Justice still fails to do what we think they ought to do?" DeWitt, who felt that things would work out, was nevertheless apprehensive about the continuing potentialities for sabotage and other subversive activities. "We know," he told Bendetsen, "that they are communicating at sea. . . ." DeWitt actually knew no such thing, as no evidence existed of such communication, but he undoubtedly believed it. Then, in a classic leap in what Richard Hofstadter has styled the paranoid style, the West Coast commander insisted that "the fact that we have had [not even] sporadic attempts at sabotage clearly means that control is being exercised somewhere." Here then was the "heads I win, tails you lose" situation in which this one Army officer was able to place more than 100,000 innocent people. There had been no acts of sabotage, no real evidence of subversion, despite the voices that DeWitt kept hearing at sea. Yet, according to this military logician, there was a conspiracy afoot not to commit sabotage until America dropped its guard. Ergo, evacuate them quickly before the conspiracy is put into operation.[11]

The next day, January 25, the long-awaited report on the attack on Pearl Harbor made by the official committee of inquiry headed by Supreme Court Justice Owen J. Roberts was released to the press just in time for the Sunday morning papers, though it is dated two days earlier. In addition to its indictment of the general conditions of unreadiness in the Hawaiian command, the board reported, falsely, as it turned out, that the attack was greatly abetted by Japanese spies, some of whom were described as "persons having no open relations with the Japanese foreign service." It went on to criticize the laxity of counterespionage activity in the Islands, and implied that a too close adherence to the Constitution had seriously inhibited the work of the Federal Bureau of Investigation.[12] The publication of the report was naturally a sensation; it greatly stimulated already prevalent rumors that linked the disaster to wholly imaginary fifth column activities by resident Japanese. Perhaps the most popular was the yarn that University of California class rings had been found on the fingers of Japanese pilots shot down in the raid. Even more ridiculous was the story that the attacking pilots had been aided by arrows, pointing at Pearl Harbor, which had been hacked into the cane fields the night before by Japanese workers. The absurdity of this device — a large natural harbor containing dozens of war vessels, large and small, is highly visible from the air — seems to have occurred to few. The Roberts Report provided a field day for those who had long urged more repressive measures and a more effective secret police unfettered by constitutional restrictions. Congressmen like Martin Dies of Texas, then head of the House Committee on Un-American Activities, insisted, in and out of Congress, that if only people had listened to them, the disaster at Pearl Harbor could have been averted. More significantly, it gave an additional argument to those who were pressing for preventive detention and must have given pause to some who had been urging restraint.

On January 25 Secretary Stimson forwarded to Attorney General Biddle recommendations that General DeWitt had made four days earlier, calling for total exclusion of enemy aliens from eighty-six Category A zones and close control of enemy aliens in eight Category B zones on a pass and permit system. As this proposal involved only aliens, the Justice Department quickly agreed and made the first public, official announcement of a mass evacuation on January 29, to be effective almost a month later, on February 24.[13] This relatively modest proposal would have moved only about 7000 aliens in all, and fewer than 3000 of these would have been Japanese. At about the same time it announced the appointment of Tom C. Clark (who later became Attorney General under Truman and then an Associate Justice of the Supreme Court) as Co-Ordinator of the Alien Enemy Control Program within the Western Defense Command. Clark flew to the West Coast the next day.

A few days before Stimson's recommendation to Biddle, the top echelons of military command, for the first time, began to become aware of the kinds of proposals that were emanating from DeWitt's headquarters. General Mark W. Clark (then a brigadier on the General Staff and later a major commander in the European Theater) was instructed to prepare a memorandum for the President on the subject of "enemy aliens" in the Western Theater of Operations. The day after Stimson's letter to Biddle requesting the announcement of Category A and B areas, General Clark recommended that no memorandum be sent unless the Attorney General's action should "not be all that is desired." Clark's memorandum was read by Chief of Staff George C. Marshall, who noted on it "hold for me until Feb. 1." The top brass was satisfied with a very modest program, involving the forced removal, without detention, of a very few aliens. Clark's memorandum made no mention of citizens at all.[14]

But if the top brass were satisfied, DeWitt, Bendetsen, and Gullion were not. And neither were the leading public officials in California. On January 27 DeWitt had a conference with Governor Culbert Olson and related to Washington, probably accurately:

> There's a tremendous volume of public opinion now developing against the Japanese of all classes, that is aliens and non-aliens, to get them off the land, and in Southern California around Los Angeles — in that area too — they want and they are bringing pressure on the government to move all the Japanese out. As a matter of fact, it's not being instigated or developed by people who are not thinking but by the best people of California. Since the publication of the Roberts Report they feel that they are living in the midst of a lot of enemies. They don't trust the Japanese, none of them.[15]

Two days later, DeWitt talked with Olson's Republican Attorney General Earl Warren. (DeWitt thought his name was Warner.) The California Attorney General, who was then preparing to run for governor against Olson in November, was in thorough agreement with his rival that the Japanese ought to be removed. This was not surprising. Warren was heir to a long anti-Japanese tradition in California politics and the protégé of U. S. Webb, a long-time Attorney General of California (1902–1939) and the author of the 1913 California Alien Land Act. Warren had been intimately associated with the most influential nativist group in the state, the Joint Immigration Committee, but shortly after he became Attorney General in 1939 he prudently arranged to have his name taken off the Committee's letterhead, although he continued to meet with them and receive copies of all documents and notices. Because of his later prominence, some have tried to make too much of Warren's very minor role in pressing for an evacuation. He did add his voice, but it was not yet a very strong one and it is almost inconceivable that, had any other politician held his post, essentially the same result would not have ensued.[16]

On the very day of Biddle's formal announcement of the A and B zones, DeWitt and Bendetsen worked out a more sweeping scheme, which Bendetsen would present to an informal but influential meeting of congressmen the next day. After a rambling conversation — DeWitt was rarely either concise or precise — Bendetsen, always the lawyer in uniform, summed it up neatly:

> BENDETSEN. . . . As I understand it, from your viewpoint summarizing our conversation, you are of the opinion that there will have to be an evacuation on the west coast, not only of Japanese aliens but also of Japanese citizens, that is, you would include citizens along with alien enemies, and that if you

had the power of requisition over all other Federal agencies, if you were requested you would be willing on the coast to accept responsibility for the
alien enemy program.

DeWitt. Yes I would. And I think it's got to come sooner or later.

Bendetsen. Yes sir, I do too, and I think the subject may be discussed tomorrow at the congressional delegation meeting.

DeWitt. Well, you've got my viewpoint. You have it exactly.[17]

The next day, January 30, the Japanese question was discussed in two important meetings, one in the White House and one on Capitol Hill. In the
Cabinet meeting fears were expressed about the potentially dangerous
situation in Hawaii. General Marshall penned a short memo to General
Dwight D. Eisenhower, then a member of his staff, telling him that Stimson
was concerned about "dangerous Japanese in Hawaii." Justice Roberts had
told the War Secretary that "this point was regarded by his board as most
serious." Several Cabinet members, but particularly Navy Secretary Frank
Knox, were greatly disturbed at what they considered the laxity with which
the Hawaiian Japanese were treated. As early as December 19, a previous
Cabinet meeting had decided that all Japanese aliens in the Hawaiian Islands should be interned, and put on some island other than Oahu, where
the major military installations were located.[18]

At the other end of Pennsylvania Avenue, the focus was on the West Coast
Japanese. Bendetsen, along with Rowe and Ennis from the Justice Department, attended a meeting of the Pacific Coast House delegation. (A joint
meeting between the congressmen and the six senators was already scheduled for the following Monday.) The subject was what to do about the Japanese. Although Bendetsen officially reported to his superiors that he "was
present as an observer," it is clear from his telephone conversations with
General DeWitt, both before and after the meeting, that he went as an advocate for the policies that he and his boss, General Gullion, had been proposing. Bendetsen called DeWitt right after the meeting and told him what
they both considered good news.

They asked me to state what the position of the War Department was. I stated
that I could not speak for the War Department. . . . They asked me for my
own views and I stated that the position of the War Department was this: that
we did not seek control of the program, that we preferred it be handled by
the civil agencies. However, the War Department would be entirely willing, I
believed, [to assume] the responsibility provided they accorded the War Department, and the Secretary of War, and the military commander under him,
full authority to require the services of any federal agency, and required that
that federal agency was required to respond.[19]

DeWitt liked this. "That's good," he responded. "I'm glad to see that action is being taken . . . that someone in authority begins to see the problem." What he particularly liked was the delegation to himself of full power over civilian agencies. He had had problems with civilians already, particularly civilians in the Federal Bureau of Investigation whose West Coast agents, as we have seen, refused to respond positively to DeWitt's imaginary alarms and excursions. As DeWitt envisioned it, "Mr. [J. Edgar] Hoover himself as head of the F.B.I. would have to function under the War Department exactly as he is functioning under the Department of Justice."

Bendetsen, naturally, encouraged DeWitt to grab for power. "Opinion is beginning to become irresistible, and I think that anything you recommend will be strongly backed up . . . by the public." DeWitt and Bendetsen agreed that protestations of loyalty from the Nisei were utterly worthless. As DeWitt put it:

> "There are going to be a lot of Japs who are going to say, 'Oh, yes, we want to go, we're good Americans and we want to go, we're good Americans and we want to do everything you say,' but those are the fellows I suspect the most."
>
> "Definitely," Bendetsen agreed. "The ones who are giving you only lip service are the ones always to be suspected."[20]

The Congressional recommendations were immediately sent to Secretary Stimson by the senior California representative, Clarence Lea, a Santa Rosa Democrat first elected in 1916. Although they did not specifically call for removal of American citizens of Japanese ancestry, the delegation did ask that mass evacuation proceed for "all enemy aliens and their families," which would have included most of the Nisei.[21] Later the same day, Provost Marshal General Gullion called DeWitt to get some details straight. He was chiefly interested in how far DeWitt proposed to move the evacuees. DeWitt did not know, but he did point out to Gullion that within California "one group wanted to move them entirely out of the state," whereas another wanted "them to be left in California." After receiving these assurances from DeWitt, Gullion began to wonder where the Army was going to put 100,000 people, and, perhaps for the first time, fleetingly realized that "a resettlement proposition is quite a proposition."[22] The following day, Bendetsen, acting for his chief, had the Adjutant General dispatch telegrams to Corps Area commanders throughout the nation asking them about possible locations for large numbers of evacuees. Bendetsen suggested some possible sites: "agricultural experimental farms, prison farms, migratory labor camps, pauper farms, state parks, abandoned CCC camps, fairgrounds."[23]

By the end of the month DeWitt was able to make his position a little clearer. When Bendetsen asked whether or not he contemplated moving citizens, DeWitt was emphatic.

I include all Germans, all Italians who are alien enemies and all Japanese who are native-born or foreign born . . . evacuate enemy aliens in large groups at the earliest possible date . . . sentiment is being given too much importance. . . . I think we might as well eliminate talk of resettlement and handle these people as they should be handled . . . put them to work in internment camps. . . . I place the following priority. . . . First the Japanese, all prices [*?sic*] . . . as the most dangerous . . . the next group, the Germans . . . the third group, the Italians. . . . We've waited too long as it is. Get them all out.[24]

On Sunday, February 1, exactly eight weeks after Pearl Harbor, Assistant Secretary of War John J. McCloy, Gullion, and Bendetsen went to a meeting in Attorney General Francis Biddle's office. Biddle, who was seconded by James Rowe, Jr., Edward J. Ennis, and J. Edgar Hoover, had been concerned about the increasing pressure for mass evacuation, both from the military and from Congress, and about a crescendo of press criticism directed at his "pussyfooting," some of which was undoubtedly inspired by the military. Biddle presented the Army men with a draft of what he hoped would be a joint press release. Its crucial sentences, which the military refused to agree to, were

The Department of War and the Department of Justice are in agreement that the present military situation does not *at this time* [my emphasis] require the removal of American citizens of the Japanese race. The Secretary of War, General DeWitt, the Attorney General, and the Director of the Federal Bureau of Investigation believe that appropriate steps have been and are being taken.

Biddle informed McCloy and the others that he was opposed to mass evacuation and that the Justice Department would have nothing to do with it. Rowe, remembering his early January visit to DeWitt's headquarters, said that the West Coast commander had been opposed to mass evacuation then and wondered what had changed his mind. According to Gullion, Rowe, after some uncomplimentary remarks about Bendetsen, complained about the hysterical tone of the protests from the West Coast, argued that the western congressmen were "just nuts" on the subject, and maintained that there was "no evidence whatsoever of any reason for disturbing citizens." Then Biddle insisted that the Justice Department would have nothing at all to do with any interference with civilians. Gullion, admittedly "a little sore," said: "Well, listen, Mr. Biddle, do you mean to tell me if the Army, the men on the ground, determine it is a military necessity to move citizens, Jap citizens, that you won't help us?"

After Biddle restated his position, McCloy, again according to Gullion, said to the Attorney General: "You are putting a Wall Street lawyer in a helluva box, but if it is a question of the safety of the country [and] the Constitution. . . . Why the Constitution is just a scrap of paper to me."

As the meeting broke up, it was agreed that the Army people would check with the "man on the ground," General DeWitt. As soon as they got back to their office, Gullion and Bendetsen made a joint phone call to the West Coast commander. They read him the proposed press release and, when the crucial sentences were reached, DeWitt responded immediately: "I wouldn't agree to that." When asked specifically whom he did want to evacuate, the answer was "those people who are aliens and who are Japs of American citizenship." Then Gullion cautioned DeWitt:

> Now I might suggest, General, Mr. McCloy was in the conference and he will probably be in any subsequent conference . . . he has not had all the benefit of conversations we have had with you — if you could give us something, not only in conversation but a written thing . . . stating your position.

DeWitt agreed to do this. Then Bendetsen summarized the Justice Department's point of view:

> . . . they say . . . if we recommend and it is determined that there should be an evacuation of citizens, they said hands off, that is the Army's job . . . they agree with us that it is possible from . . . a legal standpoint. . . . They agree with us that [the licensing theory] could be . . . the legal basis for exclusion. . . . However we insist that we could also say that while all whites could remain, Japs can't, if we think there is military necessity for that. They apparently want us to join with them so that if anything happens they would be able to say "this was the military recommendation."

DeWitt stated, "they are trying to cover themselves and lull the populace into a false sense of security."

When questioned about the details of the evacuation, DeWitt blustered: "I haven't gone into the details of it, but Hell, it would be no job as far as the evacuation was concerned to move 100,000 people."[25]

Actually, of course, it was a tremendous job, and even in such a relatively simple matter as the designation of Category A (prohibited to aliens) and Category B (restricted to aliens) zones, DeWitt's staff had botched the job. Bendetsen had to call Western Defense Command headquarters and point out that although they had permitted limited use by enemy aliens of the San Francisco–Oakland Bay Bridge (the bridge itself was Category B), all the approaches to the bridge were classified Category A, and thus prohibited.[26]

Two days after the conference in Biddle's office both Assistant Secretary of War McCloy and General George C. Marshall made separate calls to De-Witt. McCloy, and presumably Stimson and Marshall, had become concerned that DeWitt and the Provost Marshal's office were committing the Army to a policy that the policy makers had not yet agreed to. McCloy was blunt:

> . . . the Army, that means you in the area, should not take the position, even in your conversations with political figures out there [favoring] a wholesale withdrawal of Japanese citizens and aliens from the Coast. . . . We have about reached the point where we feel that perhaps the best solution of it is to limit the withdrawal to certain prohibited areas.

Then, incredibly to anyone who has read the transcripts of his conversations with Gullion and Bendetsen (which were apparently not then available to McCloy), General DeWitt denied that he had done any such thing: "Mr. Secretary . . . I haven't taken any position."[27]

This, of course, was a palpable lie. What the cautious commander knew, however, was that he had never put any recommendations on paper, and that General Gullion was not likely to produce the telephone transcripts because they showed him and his subordinates pressing for a policy that had not yet been officially sanctioned.

General Marshall's call was terse and businesslike; the extract of it which he furnished to the Secretary of War is worth quoting in full, both because of what it does and what it does not say.

> MARSHALL. Is there anything you want to say now about anything else? Of course we're on an open phone.
> DEWITT. We're on an open phone, but George I can talk a little about this alien situation out here.
> MARSHALL. Yes.
> DEWITT. I had a conference yesterday [February 2] with the Governor [Olson] and several representatives of the Department of Justice [Tom C. Clark] and the Department of Agriculture with a view to removal of the Japanese from where they are now living to other portions of the state.
> MARSHALL. Yes.
> DEWITT. And the Governor thinks it can be satisfactorily handled without having a resettlement somewhere in the central part of the United States and

removing them entirely from the state of California. As you know the people out here are very much disturbed over these aliens, and want to get them out of the several communities.

MARSHALL. Yes.

DEWITT. And I've agreed that if they can get them out of the areas limited as the combat zone, that it would be satisfactory. That would take them about 100 to 150 miles from the coast, and they're going to do that I think. They're working on it.

MARSHALL. Thank you.

DEWITT. The Department [of Justice] has a representative out here and the Department of Agriculture, and they think the plan is an excellent one. I'm only concerned with getting them away from around these aircraft factories and other places.

MARSHALL. Yes. Anything else?

DEWITT. No, that's all.

MARSHALL. Well, good luck.[28]

That same day, February 3, there was an hour-and-a-half meeting between Stimson, McCloy, Gullion, and Bendetsen. (It is not clear whether the phone conversations between McCloy and DeWitt and Marshall and DeWitt preceded, followed or straddled this meeting.) The next day Provost Marshal Gullion reported, somewhat dejectedly: ". . . the two Secretaries [Stimson and McCloy] are against any mass movement. They are pretty much against it. And they are also pretty much against interfering with citizens unless it can be done legally."[29]

What had apparently happened was that DeWitt, understanding from the McCloy and Marshall phone calls that the War Department was, as he put it, "afraid that I was going to get into a political mess," and under great pressure from Governor Olson and Tom C. Clark to allow a limited, voluntary, compromise evacuation within California, trimmed his position accordingly. Clark, a strong and vigorous personality, seemed to have great influence over the general, who described him as "a fine fellow . . . the most cooperative and forceful man I have ever had to deal with. He attacks a problem better than any civilian I have ever had contact with."[30]

Clark was clearly playing an independent role, and his position was somewhere between that of the Provost Marshal's office and that held by his own chief, the Attorney General. The plan that he sponsored or supported in the February 2 conference in Sacramento with Governor Olson and DeWitt called for a conference between Governor Olson and leading Japanese Americans which would result in a voluntary resettlement in the central valleys of California where the Japanese could augment agricultural production. As DeWitt explained the Clark-Olson plan to an unhappy Gullion:

Well, I tell you, they are solving the problem here very satisfactorily. . . . I have agreed to accept any plan they propose to put those people, Japanese Americans and Japanese who are in Category A area in the Category B area on farms. . . . We haven't got anything to do with it except they are consulting me to see what areas I will let them go into. . . . Mr. Clark is very much in favor of it . . . the people are going to handle it locally through the Governor and they are going to move those people to arable and tillable land. They are going to keep them in the state. They don't want to bring in a lot of negroes and mexicans and let them take their place. . . . They just want to put them on the land out of the cities where they can raise vegetables like they are doing now.[31]

The Provost Marshal General's men were disgusted with this turn of events. Not only were their plans being thwarted by the civilians who ran the Army — Stimson and McCloy, who were thinking in terms of creating "Japless" islands of security around a few key installations like the Consolidated-Vultee aircraft plant in San Diego, the Lockheed and North American plants in Los Angeles, and the Boeing plant in Seattle — but even their former ally, General DeWitt, the all-important man on the ground who alone could make authoritative statements about "military necessity," had now deserted their cause. As Colonel Archer Lerch, Gullion's deputy, put it:

I think I detect a decided weakening on the part of Gen. DeWitt, which I think is most unfortunate. . . . The idea suggested to Gen. DeWitt in his conference with Gov. Olson, that a satisfactory solution must be reached through a conference between the Governor and leading Jap-Americans, savors too much of the spirit of Rotary and overlooks the necessary cold-bloodedness of war.[32]

If pressure for evacuation within the Army seemed to be weakening, stronger and stronger outside forces were being brought into play. On February 2 and 3, in separate meetings, representatives and senators from all three Pacific Coast states agreed to coordinate their efforts. Serving as coordinator of these anti-Japanese efforts was Senator Hiram W. Johnson of California, who, in the mid-1920s, had masterminded a similar joint Congressional effort which brought about elimination of a Japanese quota in the Immigration Act of 1924. Johnson was actually more concerned about the defense of the West Coast — he feared a Japanese invasion — and complained bitterly to one of his political intimates that "the keenness of interest in the Japanese question far overshadowed the general proposition of our preparedness."[33]

Back in California, Governor Culbert Olson went on the air on February 4; his speech could only have further inflamed public opinion. Disseminating false information that probably came from his conference two days previously with General DeWitt and Tom Clark, he warned the already frightened people of California that

> it is known that there are Japanese residents of California who have sought to aid the Japanese enemy by way of communicating information, or have shown indications of preparation for fifth column activities.

Loyal Japanese, he insisted, could best prove their loyalty by cooperating with whatever the authorities asked them to do. Then, in a vain attempt to reassure the public, he went on to say that everything would be all right. He told of his conference with DeWitt and announced, without of course giving any specifics, that

> general plans [have been] agreed upon for the movement and placement of the entire adult Japanese population in California at productive and useful employment within the borders of our state, and under such surveillance and protection . . . as shall be deemed necessary.[34]

The next day the mayor of Los Angeles, Fletcher Bowron, outdid the governor in attempting to arouse passions. After pointing out that the largest concentration of Japanese was in Los Angeles, he turned on the venom:

> Right here in our own city are those who may spring to action at an appointed time in accordance with a prearranged plan wherein each of our little Japanese friends will know his part in the event of any possible attempted invasion or air raid.

He then argued that not only Japanese aliens but citizens of Japanese descent, some of whom were "unquestionably . . . loyal," represented a threat to Los Angeles. Disloyal Nisei, he argued, would loudly proclaim their patriotism. "Of course they would try to fool us. They did in Honolulu and in Manila, and we may expect it in California." Bowron's answer, of course, was mass internment for all Japanese, citizens and aliens alike. From favorable references to Tom Clark, he seems to have been willing to go along with the DeWitt–Olson–Clark plan of labor camps within California. Bowron also tried to take care of constitutional and ethical scruples:

> If we can send our own young men to war, it is nothing less than sickly sentimentality to say that we will do injustice to American-born Japanese to merely put them in a place of safety so that they can do no harm. . . . We [in

Los Angeles] are the ones who will be the human sacrifices if the perfidy that characterized the attack on Pearl Harbor is ever duplicated on the American continent.

In a follow-up statement the next day, Bowron put forth the interesting proposition that one of the major reasons that Japanese could not be trusted was that Californians had discriminated against them:

The Japanese, because they are unassimilable, because the aliens have been denied the right to own real property in California, because of [immigration discrimination against them], because of the marked differences in appearance between Japanese and Caucasians, because of the generations of training and philosophy that makes them Japanese and nothing else — all of these contributing factors set the Japanese apart as a race, regardless of how many generations have been born in America. Undoubtedly many of them intend to be loyal, but only each individual can know his own intentions, and when the final test comes, who can say but that "blood will tell"? We cannot run the risk of another Pearl Harbor episode in Southern California.[35]

And, that same week, in Sacramento, Attorney General Earl Warren presided over a meeting of some one hundred and fifty law enforcement officers, mostly sheriffs and district attorneys. According to a federal official who attended the meeting:

In his opening remarks, Mr. Warren cautioned against hysteria but then proceeded to outline his remarks in such a fashion as to encourage hysterical thinking. . . . Mr. [Isidore] Dockweiler, Los Angeles District Attorney . . . , asserted that the United States Supreme Court had been packed with leftist and other extreme advocates of civil liberty and that it was time for the people of California to disregard the law, if necessary, to secure their protection. Mr. Dockweiler finally worked himself into such a state of hysteria that he was called to order by Mr. Warren. . . . The meeting loudly applauded the statement that the people of California had no trust in the ability and willingness of the Federal Government to proceed against enemy aliens. One high official was heard to state that he favored shooting on sight all Japanese residents of the state.[36]

Despite relative calm in the press until the end of January, a government intelligence agency (the civilian Office of Government Reports) informed Washington that "word of mouth discussions [continue] with a surprisingly large number of people expressing themselves as in favor of sending all Japanese to concentration camps." By the end of January, the press "flared up again" with demands growing "that positive action be taken by the Federal Government. This awakening of the press has increased the verbal discussions that never ceased." By early February the *Los Angeles Times,* never friendly to the Japanese Americans, . . . could no longer find human terms to describe them. All Japanese Americans, the *Times* insisted editorially, were at least potentially enemies: "A viper is nonetheless a viper wherever the egg is hatched — so a Japanese-American, born of Japanese parents — grows up to be a Japanese, not an American."

Henry McLemore, the nationally syndicated columnist, put into words the extreme reaction against Attorney General Francis Biddle, whom Californians (probably with some prompting from the military and militant congressmen) had made the chief target of their ire. Biddle, McLemore reported, couldn't even win election as "third assistant dog catcher" in California. "Californians have the feeling," he explained, "that he is the one in charge of the Japanese menace, and that he is handling it with all the severity of Lord Fauntleroy."[37]

With this kind of encouragement in the background, Provost Marshal Gullion and his associates continued to press for mass action against the West Coast Japanese despite the fact that the officers of General Headquarters, directly under Marshall, were now trying to moderate anti-Japanese sentiment among members of Congress. On February 4, an impressive array of military personnel attended the meeting of West Coast congressmen: Admiral Harold R. Stark, Chief of Naval Operations; Brigadier General Mark W. Clark of General Headquarters (who had become Marshall's "expert" on the West Coast Japanese, even though just hours before he was to appear at the meeting he had to ask Bendetsen, "Now what is this Nisei?"); Colonel Hoyt S. Vandenberg of the Army Air Corps; and Colonel Wilton B. Persons, Chief of the (Congressional) Liaison Branch. According to Colonel Persons' report, Senator Rufus Holman of Oregon was the chief spokesman, and in pressing for an evacuation, he stressed the point that the people on the West Coast were "alarmed and terrified as to their person, their employment, and their homes." Clark then gave the congressmen the first truly military appraisal of the situation that they had received. Summarizing General Headquarters' findings, he told them that they were "unduly alarmed" and speculated that, at worst, there might be a sporadic air raid or a commando attack or two, and that while an attack on Alaska "was not a fantastic idea," there was no likelihood of a real onslaught on the West Coast states.[38]

The day after General Clark's moderate presentation, the Provost Marshal began to try to bring Assistant Secretary of War McCloy around to his point of view. On February 5 he wrote McCloy that although DeWitt had changed his mind, he (Gullion) was still of the view that mass evacuation was necessary. The DeWitt–Olson–Tom Clark idea of voluntary cooperation with Japanese American leaders, the Provost Marshal General denounced as "dangerous to rely upon. . . ." In a more detailed memo the following day (February 6) he warned McCloy of the possible grave consequences of inaction:

> If our production for war is seriously delayed by sabotage in the West Coastal states, we very possibly shall lose the war. . . . From reliable reports from military and other sources, the danger of Japanese inspired sabotage is great. . . . No half-way measures based upon considerations of economic disturbance, humanitarianism, or fear of retaliation will suffice. Such measures will be "too little or too late."

This shrewd appeal — "too little and too late" was a journalistic slogan that all too accurately described the general tenor of anti-Axis military efforts to that date — was followed by a concrete program that had been drawn up by Gullion and Bendetsen, and that the Provost Marshal General formally recommended. Somewhat short of total evacuation, it still would have involved moving the vast majority of West Coast Japanese. The plan consisted of four steps, as follows:

> *Step 1.* Declare restricted areas from which all alien enemies are barred. [This had already been done by Biddle, although it would not go into effect until February 24.]
> *Step 2.* Internment east of the Sierra Nevadas of *all* Japanese aliens, accompanied by such citizen members of their families as may volunteer for internment. [Since a majority of the Nisei were minors this would have included most of the citizen generation.]
> *Step 3.* The pass and permit system for "military reservations." [This would result, according to Gullion, in excluding citizens of Japanese extraction, "without raising too many legal questions."]
> *Step 4.* Resettlement. [Neither Gullion nor anyone else, as we shall see, had worked this out in any detail. According to the Provost Marshal General, it was "merely an idea and not an essential part of the plan."] [39]

By February 10, however, Gullion and Bendetsen, the latter now back on the West Coast to strengthen General DeWitt's resolve, seemed to have convinced McCloy, somehow, that a mass evacuation was necessary, although Secretary Stimson still clung to the idea of creating islands around strategic locations, an idea that the Provost Marshal General's men were sure he had gotten from General Stilwell. Bendetsen insisted that safety "islands" would not prevent sabotage: "if they wanted to sabotage that area, they could set the outside area on fire. They could still cut water lines and power lines." According to Bendetsen he had been over that ground twice with McCloy, who seemed to agree, and who had told Bendetsen that he would call him back after he had had another talk with the Secretary.[40]

The next day, February 11, 1942, was the real day of decision as far as the Japanese Americans were concerned. Sometime in the early afternoon, Secretary Stimson telephoned Franklin Roosevelt at the White House. Shortly after that call, McCloy phoned Bendetsen at the Presidio to tell him the good news. According to McCloy:

> . . . we talked to the President and the President, in substance, says go ahead and do anything you think necessary . . . if it involves citizens, we will take care of them too. He says there will probably be some repercussions, but it has got to be dictated by military necessity, but as he puts it, "Be as reasonable as you can."

McCloy went on to say that he thought the President would sign an executive order giving the Army the authority to evacuate. He also indicated there was at least some residual reluctance on the part of Secretary Stimson, who wanted to make a start in Los Angeles, concentrating on areas around the big bomber plants. McCloy indicated that he thought he could convince the Secretary that the limited plan was not practicable. In his conversation with McCloy, Bendetsen had talked about evacuating some 61,000 people, but in talking to Gullion about an hour later, he spoke of evacuating approximately 101,000 people.[41]

By February 11 the Provost Marshal's men had the situation all their own way. Assistant Secretary McCloy, who had been "pretty much against" their view just a week before, had been converted, and through him, Secretary Stimson and the President, although the latter probably did not take too much persuading. Bendetsen was again in San Francisco, and helping General DeWitt draft what the Western Defense commander called "the plan that Mr. McCloy wanted me to submit." Although, in retrospect, it seems clear that the struggle for mass evacuation was over by then, not all the participants knew it yet.

Among those in the dark were the staff at General Headquarters, particularly General Mark Clark who had been assigned to make the official military report on the advisability of mass evacuation. Early on February 12 he called DeWitt, and when told that an evacuation, to include citizens of Japanese descent, was in the works, he expressed disbelief. His own official memorandum, completed at about that time, had reached opposite conclusions, and deserves quoting at length, because it alone represents official military thinking on the subject.

General Clark's report concluded:

I cannot agree with the wisdom of such a mass exodus for the following reasons:

(*a*) We will never have a perfect defense against sabotage except at the expense of other equally important efforts. The situation with regards to protecting establishments from sabotage is analogous to protecting them from air attack by antiaircraft and barrage balloons. We will never have enough of these means to fully protect these establishments. Why, then, should we make great sacrifices in other efforts in order to make them secure from sabotage?

(*b*) We must weigh the advantages and disadvantages of such a wholesale solution to this problem. We must not permit our entire offensive effort to be sabotaged in an effort to protect all establishments from ground sabotage.

5. 1 recommend the following approach to this problem:

(*a*) Ascertain and designate the critical installations to be protected in each area and list them according to their importance.

(*b*) Make up our minds as to what means are available for such protection and apply that protection as far as it will go to the most critical objectives, leaving the ones of lesser importance for future consideration, or lesser protection.

(*c*) Select the most critical ones to be protected and delimit the essential areas around them for their protection.

(*d*) Eject all enemy aliens from those areas and permit entrance of others by pass only.

(*e*) Only such installations as can be physically protected in that manner should be included in this category. For example, it is practicable to do this in the case of the Boeing Plant, Bremerton Navy Yard and many other similar vital installations. In other words we are biting off a little at a time in the solution of the problem.

(*f*) Civilian police should be used to the maximum in effecting this protection.

(*g*) Federal Bureau of Investigation should be greatly augmented in counter-subversive activity.

(*h*) Raids should be used freely and frequently.

(*i*) Ring leaders and suspects should be interned liberally.

(*j*) This alien group should be made to understand through publicity that the first overt act on their part will bring a wave of counter-measures which will make the historical efforts of the vigilantes look puny in comparison.

6. It is estimated that to evacuate large numbers of this group will require one soldier to 4 or 5 aliens. This would require between 10,000 and 15,000 soldiers to guard the group during their internment, to say nothing of the continuing burden of protecting the installations. I feel that this problem

must be attacked in a sensible manner. We must admit that we are taking some chances just as we take other chances in war. We must determine what are our really critical installations, give them thorough protection and leave the others to incidental means in the hope that we will not lose too many of them — and above all keep our eye on the ball — that is, the creating and training of an offensive army.[42]

Here was truly "stern military necessity." The General Staff officer, who probably reflected Marshall's real view, would have moved very few Japanese, not because he was a defender of civil liberty, or even understood what the probabilities for sabotage really were, but because, it did not seem to him, on balance, that the "protection" which total evacuation would provide was worth its cost in military manpower and energy. But military views, as we have seen, were not the determinants of policy; political views were. The real architects of policy were the lawyers in uniform, Gullion and Bendetsen. Their most highly placed supporters, McCloy and Stimson, were two Republican, Wall Street lawyers.

Very late in the game, and often after the fact, a very few New Dealers tried to influence the President to take a more consistently democratic approach to the Japanese. On February 3 Archibald MacLeish, then Director of the Office of Facts and Figures, a predecessor of the Office of War Information, wrote one of Roosevelt's confidential secretaries suggesting that the President might want to try to hold down passions on the West Coast. His office, he said, was "trying to keep down the pressure out there." He enclosed, for the President, a statement of Woodrow Wilson's that he thought might be useful. During the other world war, Wilson had said, in a statement highly appropriate to the West Coast situation:

> . . . I can never accept any man as a champion of liberty either for ourselves or for the world who does not reverence and obey the laws of our beloved land, whose laws we ourselves have made. He has adopted the standards of the enemies of his country, whom he affects to despise.

Getting no response from the White House, MacLeish tried the Army six days later. "Dear Jack," the libertarian poet wrote McCloy, "In my opinion great care should be taken not to reach a grave decision in the present situation on the representations of officials and pressure groups alone. The decision may have far-reaching effects."[43]

MacLeish's efforts were, of course, fruitless. Much more influential was the authoritarian voice of America's chief pundit, Walter Lippmann. Writing from San Francisco in a column published on February 12, the usually detached observer who has so often been on the unpopular side of issues, was, in this instance, merely an extension of the mass West Coast mind. In an essay entitled "The Fifth Column on the Coast," Lippmann wrote:

> . . . the Pacific Coast is in imminent danger of a combined attack from within and without. . . . It is a fact that the Japanese navy has been reconnoitering the coast more or less continuously. . . . There is an assumption [in Washington] that a citizen may not be interfered with unless he has committed an overt act. . . . The Pacific Coast is officially a combat zone: Some part of it may at any moment be a battlefield. And nobody ought to be on a battlefield who has no good reason for being there. There is plenty of room elsewhere for him to exercise his rights.

The pundit's thinkpiece drew a lot of notice. Westbrook Pegler, delighted at finding a respectable man urging what he had long urged, chortled:

> Do you get what he says? This is a high-grade fellow with a heavy sense of responsibility. . . . The Japanese in California should be under armed guard to the last man and woman right now [even Pegler didn't like to talk about children] — and to hell with habeas corpus until the danger is over. . . . If it isn't true, we can take it out on Lippmann, but on his reputation I will bet it is all true.

In the War Department, Marshall sent a copy of Lippmann's column to Stimson, and Stimson sent it to McCloy, and it was undoubtedly read in the White House.[44] It was read in the Justice Department too. Long-suffering Attorney General Francis Biddle, former law clerk to Justice Holmes, civil libertarian and New Dealer, was finally stirred to respond by Lippmann's column. In his memoirs, published in 1962, deeply regretting the whole affair, Biddle wrote:

> . . . if, instead of dealing almost exclusively with McCloy and Bendetsen, I had urged [Stimson] to resist the pressure of his subordinates, the result might have been different. But I was new to the Cabinet, and disinclined to insist on my view to an elder statesman whose wisdom and integrity I greatly respected.[45]

What Biddle did not reveal, however, was that he himself had given Stimson a kind of green light. In a letter written on February 12, the Attorney General voiced his distaste for the proposed evacuation, particularly of citizens, but assured Stimson that

> I have no doubt that the Army can legally, at any time, evacuate all persons in a specified territory if such action is deemed essential from a military point

of view. . . . No legal problem arises when Japanese citizens are evacuated, but American citizens of Japanese origin could not, in my opinion, be singled out of an area and evacuated with the other Japanese.

Then Biddle, Philadelphia lawyer that he was, told Stimson how he thought it could be done.

However, the result might be accomplished by evacuating all persons in the area and then licensing back those whom the military authorities thought were not objectionable from a military point of view.[46]

Five days later, on February 17, Biddle addressed a memorandum to the President, a memorandum that was, in effect, a last-gasp effort to stop the mass evacuation that was being planned. Biddle apparently was unaware that Roosevelt had given Stimson and McCloy the go-ahead signal almost a week before. The Attorney General opened with a statement about the various West Coast pressure groups and congressmen who were urging the evacuation. He then singled out Lippmann and Pegler, and argued that their concern about imminent invasion and sabotage was not borne out by the facts. Biddle then maintained, rather curiously, that "there [was] no dispute between the War, Navy and Justice Departments," and warned that the evacuation of 93,000 Japanese in California would disrupt agriculture, require thousands of troops, tie up transportation, and raise very difficult questions of resettlement. Then, in an apparent approval of evacuation, Biddle wrote, "If complete confusion and lowering of morale is to be avoided, so large a job must be done after careful planning."

Then, in a parting blast, directed specifically at Lippmann, Biddle attacked columnists acting as "Armchair Strategists and Junior G-Men," suggested that they were essentially "shouting FIRE! in a crowded theater," and warned that if race riots occurred, Lippmann and the others would bear a heavy responsibility.[47]

But Biddle could have directed his attack much closer to home. Not only his Cabinet colleagues but some of his subordinates were doing more than shouting. Three days before the Attorney General's letter, Tom C. Clark, of his staff, assured a Los Angeles press conference that the federal government would soon evacuate over 200,000 enemy aliens and their children, including all American-born Japanese, from areas in California vital to national defense.[48]

On February 13, the Pacific Coast Congressional delegation forwarded to the President a recommendation for evacuation that was fully in line with what Stimson and McCloy were proposing. They recommended, unanimously:

the immediate evacuation of all persons of Japanese lineage and all others, aliens and citizens alike, whose presence shall be deemed dangerous or inimical to the defense of the United States from all strategic areas . . . such areas [should] be enlarged as expeditiously as possible until they shall encompass the entire strategic areas of the states of California, Oregon and Washington, and the Territory of Alaska.[49]

Finally, on Thursday, February 19, 1942, a day that should live in infamy, Franklin D. Roosevelt signed an Executive Order that gave the Army, through the Secretary of War, the authority that Gullion and Bendetsen had sought so long. Using as justification a military necessity for "the successful prosecution of the war," the President empowered the military to designate "military areas" from which "any or all persons may be excluded" and to provide for such persons "transportation, food, shelter, and other accommodations as may be necessary . . . until other arrangements are made." The words Japanese or Japanese Americans never even appear in the order; but it was they, and they alone, who felt its sting.[50]

The myth of military necessity was used as a fig leaf for a particular variant of American racism. On the very day that the President signed the order, a conference at General Headquarters heard and approved an opposite opinion. Army Intelligence reported, officially, that it believed "mass evacuation unnecessary." In this instance, at least, the military mind was superior to the political: the soldiers who opposed the evacuation were right and the politicians who proposed it were wrong. But, why did it happen?

Two major theories have been propounded by scholars which ought to be examined. Almost as the evacuation was taking place, administrators and faculty at the University of California at Berkeley took steps to set up a scholarly study of the relocation in all its aspects. With generous foundation support and with the cooperation of some of the federal officials most responsible for the decision (for example, John J. McCloy), the "Japanese American Evacuation and Resettlement Study" was set up under the directorship of Dorothy Swaine Thomas, then a University of California Professor of Rural Sociology and a skilled demographer. Her staff included a broad spectrum of social scientists, but curiously did not include either professional historians or archivists. Professor Thomas' own volumes did not seek to determine responsibility for the evacuation, but two volumes that flowed out of the project did: Morton Grodzins, *Americans Betrayed* (Chicago, 1949) and Jacobus tenBroek, Edward N. Barnhart, and Floyd Matson, *Prejudice, War, and the Constitution* (Berkeley and Los Angeles, 1954). Grodzins felt that the major cause of the evacuation was the pressure exerted by special interest groups within California and on the Pacific Coast generally. The "western group," he wrote, "was successful in having a program molded to its own immediate advantage made national policy." Professors tenBroek, Barnhart, and Matson vigorously disputed the Grodzins thesis: for them, the responsibility was General DeWitt's, and, they argued, his decision was based essentially on his "military estimate of the situation."[51]

Five years later a professional historian, Stetson Conn, then a civilian historian for the Department of the Army and later the Army's Chief of Military History, published an authoritative account of what really happened, as far as the military was concerned. He found in the contemporary evidence "little support for the argument that military necessity required a mass evacuation" and pointed, accurately, to the machinations of Gullion and Bendetsen and their success in bending the civilian heads of the War Department to their will.

The question that remains to be answered is why the recommendation of Stimson and McCloy was accepted by the nation. Grodzins' pressure groups were, of course, important, but even more important than the peculiar racism of a region was the general racist character of American society. The decision to evacuate the Japanese was popular, not only in California and the West, but in the entire nation, although only on the West Coast was it a major issue in early 1942.

The leader of the nation was, in the final analysis, responsible. It was Franklin Roosevelt, who in one short telephone call, passed the decision-making power to two men who had never been elected to any office, saying only, with the politician's charm and equivocation: "Be as reasonable as you can." Why did he agree? Probably for two reasons: in the first place, it was expedient; in the second place, Roosevelt himself harbored deeply felt anti-Japanese prejudices.

As to expediency, it is important to remember what the war news was like in early 1942. It was a very bad time for the military fortunes of the United States and its allies. The Japanese had landed on the island of Singapore on February 8, on New Britain on the 9th, and were advancing rapidly in Burma. Roosevelt was concerned, first of all with winning the war, and secondly with unity at home, so that he, unlike his former chief, Woodrow Wilson, could win the peace with the advice and consent of the Senate. He could read the Congressional signs well and knew that cracking down on the Japanese Americans would be popular both on the Hill and in the country generally. And the last thing he wanted was a rift with establishment Republicans like Stimson and McCloy; New Dealers like Biddle and MacLeish could be counted on not to rock the boat.

But, in addition, Franklin Roosevelt was himself convinced that Japanese, alien and citizen, were dangerous to American security. He, along with several members of his Cabinet and circle of advisers, persistently pushed for mass internment of the Hawaiian Japanese Americans long after the military had wisely rejected such a policy. And there was a kind of rationale for such a policy. If Japanese were a threat to security in California, where they represented fewer than 2 percent of the population, certainly in war-torn Hawaii, where they were more than a third of the population, they should have constituted a real menace. But it is one thing to incarcerate a tiny element of the population, as was done on the West Coast, and quite another to put away a sizable fraction of the whole. Apart from the sheer size of the problem, relatively and absolutely, there was the question of the disruption that such a mass evacuation would cause in the local economy. Referring to Oahu alone, Lieutenant General Delos C. Emmons, the Army commander there, pointed out to the War Department in January 1942 that Japanese provided the bulk of the main island's skilled labor force and were indispensable unless replaced by an equivalent labor force from the mainland. In addition, the logistical problems of internment in the islands were so great that Emmons recommended that any evacuation and relocation be to the mainland.

At the Cabinet level, however, different views were held. On February 27, for example, Navy Secretary Knox, the most vocal Japanophobe in the Cabinet, suggested rounding up all the Japanese on Oahu and putting them under Army guard on the neighboring island of Molokai, better known as a leper colony. Stimson concurred as to the danger, but insisted that if they were to be moved they be sent to the states. (The shipping situation, for all practical purposes, made this impossible.) The President, according to Stimson, clearly favored Knox's plan.[52] The President and his Navy Secretary, continued to press for this policy well into 1942, but eventually were forestalled by a strongly worded joint recommendation to the contrary signed by both Chief of Staff Marshall and Chief of Naval Operations Admiral Ernest J. King.[53] In other words, real rather than imaginary military necessity governed in Hawaii. Although Hawaii was the first real theater of war, fewer than 2,000 of the territory's 150,000 Japanese were ever deprived of their liberty.

Notes

1. Telephone conversation, Bendetsen and Meredith, December 7, 1941, Provost Marshal General, Record Group 389, National Archives: *Congressional Record*, 77th Cong., pp. 9603, 9808–09; see also pp. 9631 and 9958.

2. Contained in a collection of letters from Poston, Bancroft Library.

3. Stetson Conn, "The Decision to Evacuate the Japanese from the Pacific Coast," in Kent Roberts Greenfield, ed., *Command Decisions* (New York: Harcourt, 1959), p. 92.

4. Telephone conversations, Gullion and DeWitt, December 26, 1941; and DeWitt and Lerch, January 1, 1942, Stetson Conn, "Notes," Office, Chief of Military History, U.S. Army.

5. Notes on January 4, 1942, conference, Stetson Conn, "Notes."

6. Telephone conversation, McCloy and DeWitt, February 3, 1942, Assistant Secretary of War, Record Group 107, National Archives. For clarity, certain portions of McCloy's rambling conversation have been transposed. To the final remark quoted above, DeWitt responded, "Out here, Mr. Secretary, a Jap is a Jap to these people now."

7. Letters, Ford to Stimson, January 16, 1942; and Stimson to Ford, January 26, 1942, Secretary of War, Record Group 107, National Archives.

8. Memo, January 10, 1942, by J. Murray Thompson et al.

9. Letter, Wickard to Stimson, January 16, 1942, in Records of the Secretary of Agriculture, Foreign Relations 2–1. Aliens-Refugees 1942, Record Group 16, National Archives. For a fascinating glimpse of how the evacuation looked to a liberal Department of Agriculture staffer, see Laurence Hewes, *Boxcar in the Sand* (New York, 1957), pp. 151–175.

10. Sakamoto's statement enclosed in letter, William Hosokawa to Cordell Hull, January 23, 1942, Secretary of War, Record Group 107, National Archives.

11. Telephone conversation, Bendetsen and DeWitt, January 24, 1942, Provost Marshal General, Record Group 389, National Archives.

12. The entire report is published in *Pearl Harbor Attack: Hearings before the Joint Committee on the Investigation of the Pearl Harbor Attack,* Pt. 39, pp. 1–21 (Washington, 1946). The quotation is from p. 12.

13. Justice Department Press Release, January 29, 1942, in *House Report No. 2124,* 77th Cong., 2d Sess., p. 302. Thirty-two basic documents relating to the evacuation are conveniently assembled here.

14. Memo, Mark W. Clark to Deputy Chief of Staff, January 26, 1942, The Adjutant General, Record Group 407, National Archives.

15. Telephone conversation, DeWitt and Bendetsen, January 29, 1942, Provost Marshal General, Record Group 389, National Archives.

16. Telephone conversation, DeWitt and Gullion, January 30, 1942, Provost Marshal General, Record Group 389, National Archives.

17. Telephone conversation, DeWitt and Bendetsen, January 29, 1942, Provost Marshal General, Record Group 389, National Archives.

18. Memo, General Marshall to General Eisenhower, January 30, 1942, Secretary of War, Record Group 107, National Archives; Conn, "The Hawaiian Defenses after Pearl Harbor," p. 207, in Stetson Conn, Rose C. Engleman, and Byron Fairchild, *United States Army in World War II: The Western Hemisphere: Guarding the United States and Its Outposts* (Washington: Government Printing Office, 1964).

19. Telephone conversation, Bendetsen and DeWitt, January 30, 1942, Provost Marshal General, Record Group 389, National Archives.

20. Ibid.

21. Letter, Lea to Stimson, January 30, 1942, Secretary of War, Record Group 107, National Archives.

22. Telephone conversation, DeWitt and Gullion, January 30, 1942, Provost Marshal General, Record Group 389, National Archives.

23. Bendetsen, Memo for the Adjutant General, January 31, 1942, The Adjutant General, Record Group 407, National Archives.

24. Telephone conversations, DeWitt and Gullion, January 31, 1942; and DeWitt and Gullion and Bendetsen, February 1, 1942, Provost Marshal General, Record Group 389, National Archives.

25. Ibid. and telephone conversation, Gullion and Mark W. Clark, February 4, 1942, Provost Marshal General, Record Group 389, National Archives.

26. Telephone conversation, Bendetsen and Colonel Stroh, February 2, 1942, Provost Marshal General, Record Group 389, National Archives.

27. Telephone conversation, McCloy and DeWitt, February 3, 1942, Assistant Secretary of War, Record Group 107, National Archives.

28. Telephone conversation, Marshall and DeWitt, February 3, 1942, Secretary of War, Record Group 107, National Archives.

29. Telephone conversation, Gullion and Mark W. Clark, February 4, 1942, Provost Marshal General, Record Group 389, National Archives.

30. Telephone conversation, DeWitt and Bendetsen, February 7, 1942, Provost Marshal General, Record Group 389, National Archives.

31. Telephone conversation, DeWitt and Gullion, February 5, 1942, Provost Marshal General, Record Group 389, National Archives.

32. Conn, "Japanese Evacuation from the West Coast," p. 128.

33. Letters, Johnson to Rufus Holman, February 3, 1942; and Johnson to Frank P. Doherty, February 16, 1942, Johnson Mss., Pt. III, Box 19, Bancroft Library.

34. Speech text, February 4, 1942, Carton 5, Olson Mss., Bancroft Library.

35. Bowron speech and statement in *Congressional Record,* February 9, 1942, pp. A547–48.

36. Material on the meeting of law enforcement officers from California reports of the Office of Government Reports for January and February, 1942, Record Group 44, Washington National Records Center, Suitland, Md.

37. Ibid.

38. Memo for record by Persons, February 6, 1942, Stetson Conn, "Notes," Office, Chief of Military History, U.S. Army.

39. Memo, Gullion to McCloy, February 5, 1942; letter, Gullion to McCloy, February 6, 1942, Assistant Secretary of War, Record Group 107, National Archives.

40. Telephone conversation, Gullion and Bendetsen, February 10, 1942, Provost Marshal General, Record Group 389, National Archives.

41. Conn, "Japanese Evacuation from the West Coast," pp. 131–32; telephone conversations, McCloy and Bendetsen, Bendetsen and Gullion, February 11, 1942, Stetson Conn, "Notes."

42. Mark W. Clark Memo, General Headquarters, n.d. but ca. February 12, 1942, Stetson Conn, "Notes."

43. Letters, MacLeish to Grace Tully, February 3, 1942, President's Personal File 1820, Franklin D. Roosevelt Library, Hyde Park; MacLeish to McCloy, February 9, 1942, Assistant Secretary of War, Record Group 107, National Archives.

44. Lippmann column and memo slips in Secretary of War, Record Group 107, National Archives; Pegler's column, *Washington Post,* February 15, 1942, as cited in *Congressional Record,* February 17, 1942, pp. 568–69.

45. Francis B. Biddle, *In Brief Authority* (New York: Doubleday, 1962), p. 226.

46. Letter, Biddle to Stimson, February 12, 1942, Secretary of War, Record Group 107, National Archives.

47. Letter, Biddle to Franklin D. Roosevelt, February 17, 1942, Franklin D. Roosevelt Library, Hyde Park.

48. *Los Angeles Times,* February 15, 1942.

49. "Recommendations" in Assistant Secretary of War, Record Group 107, National Archives.

50. Executive Order No. 9066, February 19, 1942, in *House Report No. 2124,* 77th Cong., 2d Sess., pp. 314–15.

51. For a good summary, see Chapter IV, "Two Theories of Responsibility," pp. 185–210 in Jacobus tenBroek, Edward N. Barnhart, and Floyd W. Matson, *Prejudice, War, and the Constitution* (Berkeley and Los Angeles: University of California Press, 1954).

52. Conn, "The Hawaiian Defenses after Pearl Harbor," pp. 207–10.

53. See, for example, letter, Knox to Franklin D. Roosevelt, October 17, 1942, copy in Secretary of War, Record Group 107, National Archives; and Franklin D. Roosevelt, autograph memo to Stimson and Marshall, November 2, 1942, Secretary of War, Record Group 107, National Archives. The King-Marshall memo, July 15, 1942, is in President's Secretary File, Franklin D. Roosevelt Library, Hyde Park.

2. What caused the Supreme Court to affirm the constitutionality of internment?

Peter Irons

Gordon Hirabayashi v. United States: "A Jap's a Jap"

During Peter Irons's first year at Antioch College, his father, a nuclear engineer who helped build H-bomb plants, died. Irons would later say, "It seems probable that I had picked up from him, very indirectly, his revulsion toward nuclear weapons and his inner agony over his role in developing them." Joining a socialist discussion group and an "informal pacifist group," Irons "wound up with a Gandhian pacifism and an admiration for native American socialism and anarcho-syndicalism." After participating in a Student Nonviolent Coordinating Committee (SNCC) conference in Atlanta in 1960, he regularly picketed suburban movie theaters that discriminated against African Americans and was arrested for sitting in at a suburban Maryland bowling alley. In October 1960, the twenty-year-old Irons sent back his draft card, explaining, "I wouldn't fight as a Gandhian," and "I felt the need to make a symbolic break with a country which oppressed blacks." Later that same month, he gave a speech and distributed a pamphlet calling for a mass draft card return before the Student Peace Union at Oberlin College. Six years later, Irons went to prison for resisting the draft. After serving a twenty-six-month sentence, he was released in February 1969.[1]

The day after he got out of prison, Irons entered graduate school. After reading Howard Zinn's *SNCC: The New Abolitionists* (1965), he began corresponding with the radical scholar, who also had a history of civil rights and antiwar activism. With Zinn's help, he was accepted into the political science program at Boston University and received his Ph.D. in 1973. After graduating from Harvard Law School in 1978, he became a member of the state and federal bars. The draft protester and convict had become a lawyer and a legal historian.

The New Deal Lawyers, Peter Irons's first book, was published in 1982. A year earlier, he had begun research on the FBI for a second book. But he was dismayed to learn that the thousands of rolls of FBI microfilm were not yet indexed. Remembering the Japanese American internment cases from his law school days, he strolled over to the Library of Congress, looked up "internment" in the card catalog, and was pleased to see few recent works listed. Taking advantage of the 1976 Freedom of Information Act, Irons ordered several boxes of documents on the internment cases from the Justice Department. Originally, as he explains in the preface to *Justice at War: The Story of the Japanese American Internment Cases* (1983), he planned to write a book about lawyers:

> My focus was less on the four test case challengers or the nine Supreme Court justices than on the forty lawyers who participated on both sides of the Japanese American cases. My interest was in examining the different legal strategies and tactics these lawyers employed in wrestling with important and unsettled issues of constitutional law, viewed against a backdrop of wartime pressures and passions.

Irons never expected that his research would help rectify a wartime injustice. But as luck would have it, the first file Irons examined contained a shocking revelation: Lawyers at the Justice Department had accused their superiors of suppressing evidence and presenting to the Supreme Court a military report containing "lies" and "intentional falsehoods." Irons found evidence that Justice Department lawyers who had prepared briefs to defend internment before the Supreme Court had learned that General John L. DeWitt and other government officials knew of intelligence reports undermining their claims of "military necessity." Lawyers such as Edward Ennis and John Burling then realized that DeWitt had deliberately excluded the FBI and Naval Intelligence reports advising against internment from his Final Report. The lawyers also discovered that DeWitt knew that the Federal Communications Commission had found no evidence of Japanese Americans using radio transmitters to signal from shore to Japanese ships. Nevertheless, DeWitt had tried to justify internment with charges of "shore-to-ship signalling." Ennis and Burling considered disclosing this information to the Supreme Court, but they ultimately bowed to War Department pressure, withheld the evidence, and misrepresented their cases before the Court.

Outraged by what he deemed a "legal scandal without precedent in the history of American law," Irons contacted the three Japanese Americans — Gordon Hirabayashi, Minoru Yasui, and Fred Korematsu — who had been convicted of violating the curfew, exclusion, and internment orders during the war. After showing them this new evidence, he agreed to represent them and filed suits to reverse their criminal convictions. Irons and a team of Japanese American lawyers used an obscure provision of federal law — a "petition for a writ of error *coram nobis*"*— to reopen their cases. The lawyers charged that the original trials had been tainted by "fundamental error" and had resulted in convictions of "manifest injustice."

The selection presented here, "*Gordon Hirabayashi v. United States:* 'A Jap's a Jap,'" reviews Hirabayashi's wartime challenge of military curfew and exclusion orders and the Supreme Court decisions upholding these orders. Irons also describes how his discovery of the "suppression of evidence" before the Supreme Court caused him to urge Hirabayashi, Yasui, and Korematsu to reopen their cases in the 1980s. This account illustrates the impact scholarship and activism can have on the public record. Irons's research and Hirabayashi's effort to clear his name helped energize the movement for redress for all former internees. In 1981, both testified about their experiences before the Commission on Wartime Relocation and Internment of Civilians. The press coverage surrounding the *coram nobis* cases also aroused more public and political support for redress.

Besides *Justice at War* and *The Courage of Their Convictions* (1988; from which this selection is taken), Irons has published *Justice Delayed: The Record of the Japanese American Internment Cases* (1989). He has served two terms on the

---

coram nobis: an order by a court of appeals to a court that rendered judgment requiring the trial court to consider facts not in the trial record that might have resulted in a different judgment if known at the time of the trial.

national board of the American Civil Liberties Union and is currently a professor of political science and director of the Earl Warren Bill of Rights Project. Like Roger Daniels, he continues to remind all Americans of the injustice of Japanese American internment in speeches, articles, books, and historical exhibits.

Gordon Hirabayashi served an eighty-day sentence following his conviction for violation of the curfew and exclusion orders in 1942. Afterward, he continued his college studies, specializing in sociology. He received a bachelor's degree in 1946, a master's degree in 1949, and a Ph.D. in 1952, all from the University of Washington. His first teaching job was at the American University of Beirut, where he served as chair of the sociology department. He later served as assistant director of the Social Research Center and headed the Department of Sociology and Anthropology at the American University in Cairo. In 1959, he accepted a position at the University of Alberta, where he served as the longtime chair of the Department of Sociology and Anthropology. A pioneer in Canadian ethnic studies, he helped develop the social sciences in Alberta and throughout Canada. Now retired, he continues to speak about his case, redress, and other human rights issues to groups across North America.

Questions for a Closer Reading

1. Why did Gordon Hirabayashi decide to defy the curfew and exclusion orders? What would you have done if you had been in his position in 1942?

2. How did Judge Lloyd Black and the members of the U.S. Supreme Court justify their decisions in Hirabayashi's case and the cases of the other wartime challengers? How did these decisions affect views of military authority, due process, and constitutional rights?

3. Imagine that Justice Department lawyers such as Edward Ennis provided full disclosure of the evidence they found to the Supreme Court. What impact do you think this might have had on the Court's decision?

4. Gordon Hirabayashi wrote an essay titled "Am I an American?" Compare the way the courts answered this question in 1943 and 1987. What changes in American society, cul-

ture, and politics might explain these different definitions of what it means to be an "American"?

5. Peter Irons's research changed Hirabayashi's life. Do you think this situation reflects the potential for historical scholarship to affect contemporary lives, or was it an unusual case? Explain.

Note

1. Michael Ferber and Staughton Lynd, *The Resistance* (Boston: Beacon Press, 1971), pp. 12–13.

Gordon Hirabayashi v. United States: "A Jap's a Jap"

On the morning of May 16, 1942, Gordon Kiyoshi Hirabayashi arrived at the FBI office in Seattle, Washington. Somewhat formal in demeanor, the University of Washington senior shook hands with Special Agent Francis V. Manion and introduced his companion, Arthur Barnett, a young lawyer and fellow member of Seattle's Quaker community. Five days earlier, Gordon had defied a military order that required "all persons of Japanese ancestry" to register for evacuation to the state fairground at Puyallup, south of Seattle. From this temporary home, where Army troops herded them into cattle stalls and tents, the uprooted Japanese Americans would be shipped to "relocation centers" in desolate areas of desert or swampland, from California to Arkansas. Forced into exile, more than 120,000 Americans of Japanese ancestry endured wartime internment in America's concentration camps, housed in tarpaper barracks and guarded by armed soldiers.

After a few minutes of small talk, Gordon handed Agent Manion a neatly typed four-page document, headed "Why I refused to register for evacuation." Gordon's statement reflected his anguish as a Quaker volunteer over

Peter Irons, *Gordon Hirabayashi v. United States:* "A Jap's a Jap," in *The Courage of Their Convictions,* ed. Peter Irons (New York: The Free Press, 1988), 37–62.

moving evacuees to the Puyallup fairground. "This order for the mass evacuation of all persons of Japanese descent denies them the right to live," he wrote. "It forces thousands of energetic, law-abiding individuals to exist in a miserable psychological, and a horrible physical, atmosphere." Gordon pointed out that native-born American citizens like himself constituted a majority of the evacuees, yet their rights "are denied on a wholesale scale without due process of law and civil liberties." His statement ended on a defiant note: "If I were to register and cooperate under those circumstances, I would be giving helpless consent to the denial of practically all of the things which give me incentive to live. I must maintain my Christian principles. I consider it my duty to maintain the democratic standards for which this nation lives. Therefore, I must refuse this order for evacuation."

After reading the statement, Manion reminded Gordon that he risked a year's imprisonment for his stand. Gordon remained adamant, even after Manion drove him to the registration center and offered a last chance to sign the forms. When they returned to the FBI office, Manion conferred with the U.S. attorney, who then filed criminal charges against Gordon for violating the evacuation order.

After placing his prisoner in the King County jail, Manion dug into Gordon's briefcase and discovered a diary that confessed his violation of the military curfew orders that kept Japanese Americans off the streets in the weeks before evacuation. "Peculiar, but I receive a lift — perhaps it is a release — when I consciously break the silly old curfew," Gordon wrote one night after escorting his friend Helen Blom to her home. Manion reported his find to the U.S. attorney, who promptly filed an additional criminal charge against Gordon for curfew violation.

The wartime internment of Japanese Americans began soon after the Japanese attack on Pearl Harbor of December 7, 1941. After an initial period of tolerance and press reminders that most residents of Japanese ancestry were "good Americans, born and educated as such," public pressure mounted for their mass removal from coastal states. Fueled by past decades of "Yellow Peril" agitation, and current fears of a follow-up "sneak attack" upon the American mainland, this campaign enlisted politicians and pundits. Los Angeles congressman Leland Ford urged in mid-January, 1942, that "all Japanese, whether citizens or not, be placed in inland concentration camps." The next month, right-wing columnist Westbrook Pegler demanded that Japanese Americans be placed "under armed guard to the last man and woman right now — and to hell with habeas corpus until the danger is over."

Despite these incendiary appeals, federal officials charged with protecting the Pacific coast from sabotage and espionage saw no reason for mass evacuation. Acting on orders from Attorney General Francis Biddle, FBI agents arrested more than two thousand Japanese aliens in the days after Pearl Harbor. Justice Department officers conducted individual loyalty hearings for this group; most were promptly released and returned to their families. The FBI also investigated hundreds of Army reports of signals to enemy submarines off the coast by lights or illicit radios, and dismissed each report as unfounded. FBI director J. Edgar Hoover reported that "the army was getting a bit hysterical" in blaming the phantom lights on Japanese Americans.

Attorney General Biddle, with Hoover's reports in hand, assured President Franklin Roosevelt on February 7 that Army officials had offered "no reasons for mass evacuation" as a military measure. Secretary of War Henry Stimson, a respected elder statesman in Roosevelt's wartime cabinet, shared Biddle's concerns: "We cannot discriminate among our citizens on the ground of racial origin," Stimson wrote in early February. Any forced removal of Japanese Americans, he noted, would tear "a tremendous hole in our constitutional system." Stimson felt that internment on racial grounds would conflict with the Due Process clause of the Fifth Amendment, which required formal charges and trial before any person could be deprived of "liberty" and confined by the government.

Within days of these statements, Biddle and Stimson capitulated to the advocates of internment. Three of Stimson's War Department subordinates combined to overcome his constitutional qualms. Stimson had asked his deputy, John J. McCloy, to frame a "final recommendation" on the treatment of Japanese Americans. McCloy, who scornfully dismissed the Constitution as "a piece of paper" which military officials could tear into shreds, later defended the internment as "retribution" for the Japanese attack on Pearl Harbor.

Colonel Karl Bendetsen, the young lawyer whom McCloy had delegated to draft the report to Stimson, exemplified the persistence of racial stereotypes: "The Japanese race is an enemy race," Bendetsen wrote over the signature of General John L. DeWitt, the West Coast Army commander. Even among those born in the United States, Bendetsen argued, "the racial strains are undiluted." General DeWitt hardly bothered to mask his racial prejudice. Regardless of citizenship, DeWitt bluntly told a congressional panel, "a Jap's a Jap."

The fate of Japanese Americans was sealed at a showdown meeting on February 17, 1942. McCloy and Bendetsen presented Attorney General Biddle with a proposed presidential order, providing that "any or all persons may be excluded" from their homes on military order. Biddle's deputy, Edward Ennis, heatedly opposed the War Department proposal on constitutional grounds, but arguments of "military necessity" finally persuaded the Attorney General. Two days later, President Roosevelt signed Executive

Order 9066 and General DeWitt assigned Colonel Bendetsen to implement the evacuation and internment plans.

Gordon Hirabayashi languished in the King County jail for five months before his trial on October 20, 1942. Judge Lloyd Black, a former state prosecutor and American Legion post commander, had already dismissed the constitutional challenge filed by Gordon's trial lawyer, Frank Walters, who argued that the Constitution barred any form of racial discrimination. Rejecting this "technical interpretation" of the Fifth Amendment, Black answered that individual rights "should not be permitted to endanger all of the constitutional rights of the whole citizenry" during wartime. Judge Black added a large dose of racism to his opinion. Branding the Japanese as "unbelievably treacherous and wholly ruthless," he conjured up "suicide parachutists" who would drop from the skies onto Seattle's aircraft factories. Black predicted that these airborne invaders would seek "human camouflage and with uncanny skill discover and take advantage of any disloyalty among their kind." The military curfew and evacuation orders, he concluded, were reasonable protections against the "diabolically clever use of infiltration tactics" by potential Japanese saboteurs.

After this opinion, Gordon's trial became a perfunctory exercise. Gordon admitted his intentional violation of the curfew and evacuation orders, and explained to the all-male, elderly jurors his belief that "I should be given the privileges of a citizen" under the Constitution, regardless of his race or ancestry. The government prosecutor, Allen Pomeroy, called Gordon's father as a prosecution witness, hoping that his halting English would remind the jurors of Gordon's ties to the Japanese enemy. Gordon's parents, brought to court from a California internment camp, spent two weeks in the King County jail on Judge Black's order.

After the trial testimony ended, Frank Walters told the jurors that "I am not representing a man who violated a valid law of the United States" and restated his attack on the racial basis of the military orders. Asking the jurors to convict Gordon, Allen Pomeroy reminded them of his Japanese ancestry and warned that "if we don't win this war with Japan there will be no trial by jury."

Judge Black sent the jurors to their deliberations with an instruction that the military orders were "valid and enforceable" laws. Whether Gordon had violated the orders was the only question for decision. Black answered for the jurors, telling them that "you are instructed to return a finding of guilty" on both criminal counts. The dutiful jurors returned in ten minutes with the proper verdicts, and Black sentenced Gordon to concurrent sentences of three months in jail for each conviction. Frank Walter stated his intention to appeal the convictions, and Gordon returned to jail after Judge Black denied his request for release on bail until the appeal was decided.

Before the U.S. Court of Appeals met in San Francisco to hear Gordon's appeal, two other internment challenges reached the appellate judges. Minoru Yasui, a young Oregon lawyer and Army reserve officer, had been convicted of curfew violation and sentenced to the maximum term of one year in jail. Before his trial, Yasui had spent nine months in solitary confinement. Fred Korematsu, a shipyard welder in the San Francisco area, had volunteered for Navy service before the Pearl Harbor attack but was rejected on medical grounds. Korematsu evaded the evacuation order for two months, hoping to remain with his Caucasian fiancée, but was caught and sentenced to a five-year probationary term in an internment camp.

The Court of Appeals met for argument on the three cases on February 19, 1943, the first anniversary of President Roosevelt's internment order. Five weeks later, the appellate judges sent the cases to the Supreme Court without decision, under the little-used procedure of "certification" of questions,* over the protest of Judge William Denman, who denounced the "war-haste" with which the cases were being rushed to judgment. Denman's colleagues confessed that the question of "whether this exercise of the war power can be reconciled with traditional standards of personal liberty and freedom guaranteed by the Constitution, is most difficult."

Before the Supreme Court met to consider the cases, government lawyers fought a spirited, but unseen, battle over the evidence the justices should consider in making their decision. Solicitor General Charles Fahy delegated the task of preparing the government's briefs to Edward Ennis, who had earlier waged a futile battle against internment. During his preparation, Ennis discovered an official report of the Office of Naval Intelligence on the loyalty of Japanese Americans. Prepared by Kenneth Ringle, a Navy commander who spoke fluent Japanese, this lengthy report concluded that "less than three percent" of the entire group posed any potential threat and noted that FBI agents had already arrested most of these suspects. The Ringle report, circulated to Army officials before the evacuation began, urged that Japanese Americans be given individual loyalty hearings and that mass internment be avoided.

Ennis recognized the significance of this document and promptly informed Solicitor General Fahy that the government had "a duty to advise the Court of the existence of the Ringle memorandum" and the Army's knowledge of its conclusions. "It occurs to me that any other course of conduct might approximate the suppression of evidence," Ennis warned his superior. Fahy ignored this red-flag request.

---

* *"certification of questions":* Method of taking a case from the U.S. Court of Appeals to the Supreme Court in which a former court may certify any question of law in any civil or criminal case as to which instructions are requested.

When the Supreme Court convened on May 10, 1943, Fahy suggested that doubts about the loyalty of Japanese Americans had justified the military curfew and evacuation orders. These doubts made it "not unreasonable" for military officials "to fear that in case of an invasion there would be among this group of people a number of persons who might assist the enemy." Having planted the seed of genetic guilt, Fahy left it to germinate in the minds of the nine justices.

Just a week before meeting to decide the internment cases, the justices had issued bitterly divided opinions in the *Barnette* flag-salute case. Voiding the expulsion from public schools of Jehovah's Witnesses who objected on religious grounds to compulsory flag-salute laws, the Supreme Court majority had overturned its *Gobitis* decision, issued in 1940. Chief Justice Harlan Fiske Stone, who succeeded Charles Evans Hughes in 1941, hoped to heal the wounds of this fratricidal battle and urged his colleagues to join a unanimous opinion in the internment cases. The justices had earlier returned the Korematsu case to the court of appeals for decision on a technical issue, and the Yasui case was complicated by the trial judge's ruling that the defendant had lost his American citizenship. Gordon Hirabayashi's appeal thus became the vehicle for weighing "war powers" against "due process" in the constitutional scale.

Speaking first at the conference table, Stone placed a heavy thumb on the scale. Admitting that the military orders imposed "discrimination" on American citizens on racial grounds, he suggested that the Pearl Harbor attack showed the "earmarks of treachery" among Japanese Americans. Military officials had simply responded to the "grave danger" of sabotage and espionage by "disloyal members" of this minority. Stone also convinced his colleagues to leave the more troublesome evacuation issue for later decision. Only Justice Frank Murphy reserved his decision when Stone polled the court; every other justice voted to sustain Gordon's conviction for curfew violation.

The Chief Justice assumed the task of writing for the court, hoping to put his prestige behind the decision. Stone acknowledged that racial discrimination was "odious to a free people" and had "often been held to be a denial of equal protection" by the Supreme Court. During wartime, however, "the successful prosecution of the war" may justify measures which "place citizens of one ancestry in a different category from others." Stone suggested that Japanese Americans had failed to become "an integral part of the white population" and stressed their "attachments to Japan and its institutions." Stone's evidence for these assertions included "irritation" at laws that barred Japanese immigrants from American citizenship and the fact that many children attended "Japanese language schools" to maintain their cultural heritage. Military officials who feared a "fifth column" of disloyal

Japanese Americans were entitled, Stone concluded, to impose a curfew on "residents having ethnic affiliations with an invading enemy."

Before the Hirabayashi opinion was issued, Frank Murphy wrote a scathing dissent from Stone's racial assumptions. The court's only Catholic, Murphy noted that many immigrants sent their children to parochial and foreign-language schools, without any loss of loyalty. The issue to Murphy was not the curfew but "the gigantic round-up" of American citizens, in which he found "a melancholy resemblance to the treatment accorded to members of the Jewish race" by America's wartime enemies. This reference to Nazi concentration camps upset Justice Felix Frankfurter, who warned Murphy that any dissent would be "playing into the hands of the enemy." Faced with this appeal to patriotism, Murphy withdrew his dissent and filed a concurring opinion that placed the curfew order on "the very brink of constitutional power."

Eighteen months later, when the Supreme Court met to decide the Korematsu case, the tides of war had shifted and the continued detention of Japanese Americans struck many — including Army officials — as unnecessary. Nonetheless, Justice Hugo Black wrote for six members of the Court in upholding General DeWitt's evacuation orders. Black took pains to deny that Fred Korematsu's treatment reflected "hostility to him or his race," holding that it was based on "evidence of disloyalty" among Japanese Americans. One of the three dissenters, Justice Robert Jackson, disparaged Black's "evidence" as nothing more than the "self-serving statement" of General De-Witt, whose official report on the internment program had labeled Japanese Americans as members of an "enemy race." Justice Murphy revised his reluctant concurrence in the Hirabayashi case into an impassioned dissent in the Korematsu case. The forced exclusion of American citizens from their homes, Murphy wrote, "goes over 'the very brink of constitutional power' and falls into the ugly abyss of racism."

The surrender of Japan in 1945 did not end the internment of Japanese Americans: More than a year passed before the last concentration camp closed its gates. Slowly and fearfully, members of this "disloyal" minority returned to their homes, although many left the Pacific coast for new lives in the Midwest and East. Beginning in most cases from scratch, the former prisoners opened stores and farms, and sent their children to prestigious colleges and to success in business and professional careers. But the psychic scars of internment remained.

Four decades passed before Japanese Americans found a collective voice for their wartime trauma. Pressed by young people who joined the civil-rights and anti-war movements of the sixties and seventies, survivors of the concentration camps abandoned the Japanese tradition of "gaman" — "keep it inside"— and shared their feelings of hurt and shame. Moving from personal anguish to political action, Japanese Americans organized a "redress" movement and persuaded Congress in 1981 to establish a blue-ribbon panel to review the internment program and propose remedies for legal wrongs. After hearing testimony, often tearful, from 750 witnesses, and reviewing thousands of government documents, the Commission on Wartime Relocation and Internment of Civilians agreed that the internment "was not justified by military necessity" but had resulted from "race prejudice, war hysteria and a failure of political leadership." With only one dissent, the commissioners asked Congress to provide compensation of $20,000 for each internment survivor.

Another goal of the redress movement was to secure judicial reversal of the criminal convictions the Supreme Court had upheld in 1943 and 1944. Research by commission staff members and Peter Irons, a lawyer and legal historian, uncovered federal records that disclosed the "suppression of evidence" to the courts and the racist basis of the mass internment. After he showed these records to Gordon Hirabayashi, Minoru Yasui, and Fred Korematsu, Irons secured their agreement to reopen their cases through the little-used legal procedure of *coram nobis,** available only to criminal defendants whose trials had been tainted by "fundamental error" or "manifest injustice."

Aided by teams of volunteer lawyers, most of them children of former internees, Irons drafted *coram nobis* petitions which were filed in January 1983 with federal courts in Seattle, Portland, and San Francisco. Based entirely on government records, the lengthy petitions asked the courts to vacate the wartime convictions and make judicial findings on the government's misconduct. The government answered the petitions with a two-page response which labeled the internment as an "unfortunate episode" in American history. Although government lawyers denied any misconduct, they did not challenge the charges of suppressing crucial evidence.

The Korematsu case became the first to reach decision, in October 1983. After hearing lawyers on both sides, Judge Marilyn Patel asked Fred Korematsu to address the court. "As long as my record stands in federal court," he quietly stated, "any American citizen can be held in prison or concentration camps without a trial or a hearing." Ruling from the bench, Judge Patel labeled the government's position as "tantamount to a confession of error" and erased Fred's conviction from the court's records. Ruling in January 1984, Judge Robert Belloni of the federal court in Portland, Oregon, vacated Minoru Yasui's conviction, although he declined to make findings on the petition's misconduct charges.

*See note p. 67.

Gordon Hirabayashi waited until June 1985 for a hearing on his petition. By this time, government lawyers had decided to defend the wartime internment. Judge Donald Voorhees presided at the two-week hearing in the same Seattle courthouse in which Gordon was tried in 1942. Government lawyer Victor Stone called a parade of former FBI and intelligence officials to support claims that General DeWitt's wartime orders were "rational" responses to threats of espionage and sabotage. One official labeled Japanese Americans as "the most likely friends of the enemy" and another recalled "espionage nets" along the Pacific coast. Under examination by Gordon's lawyers, none of the government witnesses could point to a single documented instance of wartime espionage by Japanese Americans.

The star witness at Gordon's hearing was Edward Ennis, the former Justice Department lawyer who had objected to the "suppression of evidence" before the Supreme Court in 1943. Four decades later, Ennis repeated his objections and stated that John McCloy and Karl Bendetsen of the War Department had "deceived" him about the Army's false espionage charges. These wartime actions, Voorhees ruled in February 1986, constituted "error of the most fundamental character" and required vacation of Gordon's conviction for violating DeWitt's evacuation order. However, Voorhees described the curfew as a "relatively mild" restriction and upheld Gordon's conviction on this count.

Neither side was satisfied with this Solomonic outcome, the mirror image of the Supreme Court decisions of 1943, and both sets of lawyers filed appeals of Judge Voorhees' rulings. After hearing arguments and reading lengthy briefs, a three-judge panel of the Ninth Circuit Court of Appeals issued a unanimous opinion on September 24, 1987. Judge Mary Schroeder wrote for the court, concluding from the evidence presented to Judge Voorhees, that "General DeWitt was a racist" and that his military orders were "based upon racism rather than military necessity." Disagreeing with Judge Voorhees that "the curfew was a lesser restriction on freedom" than evacuation, the appellate judges vacated Gordon's remaining criminal conviction.

Government lawyers conceded defeat after this blunt rebuff and declined to file a final appeal with the Supreme Court. Gordon Hirabayashi, a college student in 1942 and now an emeritus professor, credited his victory to the new generation of Japanese Americans. "I was just one of the cogs" in the crusade for vindication, he reflected. "This was truly the people's case."

3. Why did U.S. officials intern people of Japanese ancestry from Central and South America?

Michi Weglyn

Hostages

As a Nisei teenager during World War II, Michi Nishiura Weglyn trusted President Franklin Roosevelt's rationale that internment was in the best interests of the country. Even though she contracted tuberculosis at the Gila River camp, Weglyn didn't resent the government for putting her behind barbed wire. In the preface to *Years of Infamy: The Untold Story of America's Concentration Camps* (1976), Weglyn recalls her feelings during the war. Like many young internees, she blamed herself rather than the government and wanted to eradicate "the stain of dishonor we collectively felt for the treachery of Pearl Harbor." Internment, Weglyn believed, "was the only way to prove our loyalty to a country which we loved with the same depth of feeling that children in Japan were then being brought up to love their proud island nation."

Twenty-five years later, Weglyn reconsidered her views of internment and out of curiosity began examining archival documents. "Among once impounded papers," she came "face to face with facts" that left her "greatly pained." She spent seven years conducting research at the National Archives, the Library of Congress, and the Pentagon. Sometimes the revelations made her physically sick for days. Weglyn describes this period of the late 1960s and early 1970s, when stories of protest against the Vietnam War and the Watergate break-in and cover-up filled the news, as a time when "angry charges of government duplicity and 'credibility gaps' were being hurled at heads of state." Her research convinced her that "the gaps of the evacuation era appeared more like chasms." She resolved to write a book when she heard this statement by Attorney General Ramsey Clark claim "We have never had, do not now have and will not ever have concentration camps here."[1] She felt a responsibility to "those whose honor was so wrongly impugned, many of whom died without vindication." At first, publishers praised Weglyn's scholarship but called her book, *Years of Infamy,* "objectionable" because of its harsh indictment of government leaders. According to Weglyn, William Morrow published the book in 1976 because the climate had changed with Watergate and the Pentagon Papers.

This selection from *Years of Infamy* draws attention to the little-known plight of Latin Americans of Japanese ancestry whom the U.S. government interned to exchange for Americans held captive by the Japanese. Using letters, memos, and other official records, Weglyn documents the State Department's role in transporting and imprisoning 2,264 people of Japanese ancestry from Central and South America. Why was the State Department interested in Japanese Latin Americans? By early 1942, the United States and Japan had begun negotiating to exchange nationals, both officials and private citizens, imprisoned by both sides. State Department officials used Japanese Latin Americans for these exchanges, sending 1,100 of them to Japan in July 1942 and another 1,300 in September 1943.

Twelve Latin American countries sent people of Japanese ancestry to U.S. camps, but 80 percent of them came from Peru. Due to a long history of economic competition and cultural prejudice, the Peruvian government wanted to expel all Japanese nationals from the country. Technically, the United States approved the removal of only "dangerous" enemy aliens, but the program was remarkably arbitrary, and both Japanese immigrants and Peruvian citizens of Japanese ancestry were often seized for no apparent reason. Some were deported in place of wealthy Japanese Peruvians who had bribed the police. John Emmerson, third secretary of the American Embassy in Peru, who helped compile the deportation lists, later acknowledged, "During my period of service in the embassy, we found no reliable evidence of planned or contemplated acts of sabotage, subversion, or espionage."[2]

Japanese Latin Americans were not sent to the camps run by the War Relocation Authority (WRA), which held most of the Japanese Americans from the West Coast. Instead, like the "enemy aliens" rounded up by the FBI after Pearl Harbor, they were sent to camps run by the Justice Department and were treated as prisoners of war. Compounding the injustice, the U.S. government made sure that Japanese Latin Americans were classified as "illegal aliens" when they entered the country, even though their passports and visas had been confiscated en route to America. This designation paved the way for the United States to deport these people to Japan after the war. Many Japanese Latin Americans did not want to go to Japan, a country devastated by war and a land many of them had never seen. In this selection, Weglyn shows how such individuals chose to fight deportation through the courts and were able to remain in the United States.

Many former internees first learned about government racism and misconduct during the war from Weglyn's *Years of Infamy*. Activist Raymond Okamura hailed the way Weglyn, a "theatrical designer with no historical training," found an "astonishing number of facts previously de-emphasized, ignored, or censored." Crediting her with shattering the "previous image of WRA-benevolence-inmate cooperation," Okamura pronounced the book a "major breakthrough for the telling of Japanese American history from a Japanese American perspective."[3] In addition, Weglyn's book gave many Japanese Americans the courage to speak out publicly about their experiences. In a review published in the *Pacific Citizen* on February 6, 1976, Mary Karasawa described how she felt the "need to really talk" about internment after she finished reading the book:

> I don't think anyone who lived through the "camp experience" will be able to finish reading this book without experiencing every range of human emotion — much of which has been lying dormant for the past 30 years. . . . You will swear, you will cry, you will feel bitter, but you will surely begin to see the pieces of the puzzle come together.[4]

Years of Infamy also helped stimulate redress activism throughout the country. In 1976, the Japanese American Citizens League (JACL) gave Weglyn its Biennium Award and praised the way her book "therapeutically expiates the demon of shame and guilt among Japanese Americans." The league also noted that her "extensive documentation is a valuable resource in JACL's effort to realize reparations legislation." Throughout the history of the redress movement, leaders of various factions have paid tribute to Weglyn for inspiring their activism. After receiving many letters that thanked her for reviving memories of the camps, Weglyn publicly urged "all who have lived in shame and silence for many years" to "begin to speak more openly" about the "government's crimes . . . so that it can never happen again."[5] During the 1970s and 1980s, increasing numbers of former internees responded to Weglyn's call, culminating in the testimony of more than five hundred Japanese Americans at the Commission on Wartime Relocation and Internment of Civilians hearings in 1981.

Weglyn continued to fight for the forgotten victims of internment after passage of the 1988 redress legislation, which excluded Japanese Latin Americans. She publicly denounced government claims that Japanese Latin Americans were ineligible because of their "illegal alien" status or because responsibility for their plight lay with the Latin American governments. Her research and advocacy helped fuel the *Mochizuki* class action lawsuit, which led the government in 1999 to offer a settlement of $5,000 to each surviving Japanese Latin American. Although this amount was far short of the $20,000 paid to Japanese American internees, it at least acknowledged U.S. culpability in their internment.

Long considered a leader of the Japanese American community in New York City, Weglyn was awarded an honorary doctorate from Hunter College in June 1990 for her contributions to the Asian American community. In June 1993, California State Polytechnic University at Pomona established an endowed chair, the Michi and Walter Weglyn Chair for Multicultural Studies, in honor of the Weglyns. In February 1998, academics, politicians, and activists in Los Angeles presented her with the Fighting Spirit Award for her work on behalf of Japanese Americans. When Michi

Weglyn passed away on April 25, 1999, at the age of seventy-two, services were held throughout the country to commemorate her community service.

Questions for a Closer Reading

1. Weglyn begins the selection by speculating that officials may have viewed Japanese Latin Americans as a "reprisal reserve" for Americans mistreated by the Japanese. Do you think this is plausible? Why or why not?

2. Weglyn provides a global perspective on internment. Compare the motives and policies of Canada, Latin America, Alaska, and the rest of the United States. Within the United States, how did the internment experience in a Justice Department camp compare with the experience in a WRA camp?

3. Why did the State Department and the Justice Department work together to try to deport Japanese Latin Americans at the end of the war? How was this countered by the internees and by Wayne Collins?

4. The Commission on Wartime Relocation and Internment of Civilians called the history of Japanese Latin Americans "one of the strange, unhappy, largely forgotten stories of World War II." Yet the commission did not propose redress for Japanese Latin Americans, who were excluded from redress legislation. Do you agree with this decision? Why or why not? If you were a former internee offered the government's settlement of $5,000, would you take it or continue to fight in court? Could you use the research in this article to bolster your claims?

5. Japanese American activists praised Weglyn for providing a Japanese American perspective on the history of internment. Why do you think this research by a former internee might have helped Japanese Americans break their decades of silence about the wartime incarceration?

Notes

1. *The Sacramento Bee,* June 27, 1976.
2. Commission on Wartime Relocation and Internment of Civilians, *Personal Justice Denied: Report of the Commission on Wartime Relocation and Internment of Civilians* (Washington, D.C.: US Government Printing Office, 1982), p. 314.

3. Raymond Okamura, "The Concentration Camp Experience from a Japanese American Perspective," *Counterpoint: Perspectives on Asian America,* ed. Emma Gee (Los Angeles: Asian American Studies Center, University of California at Los Angeles, 1976), p. 30.

4. *Pacific Citizen,* February 6, 1976.

5. *Hokubei Mainichi,* May 19, 1976.

Hostages

I'm for catching every Japanese in America, Alaska, and Hawaii now and putting them in concentration camps. . . . Damn them! Let's get rid of them now!

— CONGRESSMAN JOHN RANKIN,
Congressional Record, December 15, 1941

1.

Since much of Munson's documentation for the President* reads more like a tribute to those of Japanese ancestry than a need for locking them up, the question remains: Had the President, having perceived the racist character of the American public, deliberately acquiesced to the clearly punitive action knowing it would be rousingly effective for the flagging home-front morale?

Or could factors other than political expedience, perhaps a more critical wartime exigency, have entered into and inspired the sudden decision

---

*Weglyn is referring to what historians have called the "Munson Report," a secret government intelligence report on the loyalty of Japanese Americans delivered to President Roosevelt, the State Department, the War Department, and the Navy in early November 1941. Curtis B. Munson, a successful Chicago businessman, posed as a government official to gather information from FBI and Naval Intelligence sources for an informal intelligence system developed for President Roosevelt. The report concluded, "For the most part the local Japanese are loyal to the United States, or at worst, hope that by remaining quiet they can avoid concentration camps or irresponsible mobs. We do not believe that they would be at least any more disloyal than any other racial group in the United States with whom we went to war."

Michi Weglyn, "Hostages," in *Years of Infamy: The Untold Story of America's Concentration Camps* (New York: Morrow Quill Paperbacks, a Division of William Morrow and Company, Inc., 1976), 54–66.

calling for mass action — made as it was at a time when the Allied cause in the Pacific was plummeting, one reversal following another in seemingly endless succession?

A bit of personal conjecture: Shocked and mortified by the unexpected skill and tenacity of the foe (as the Administration might have been), with America's very survival in jeopardy, what could better insure the more considerate treatment of American captives, the unknown thousands then being trapped daily in the islands and territories falling to the enemy like dominoes, than a substantial *hostage reserve?* And would not a readily available *reprisal reserve* prove crucial should America's war fortune continue to crumble: should the scare propaganda of "imminent invasion" become an actual, living nightmare of rampaging hordes of yellow "barbarians" overrunning and making "free fire zones" of American villages and hamlets — looting, raping, murdering, slaughtering. . . .

In an earlier crisis situation which had exacerbated U.S.-Japan relations to the near-breaking point, the very sagacity of such a contingency plan had been forthrightly brought to the attention of the President by Congressman John D. Dingell of Michigan. On August 18, 1941, months before the outbreak of hostilities, the Congressman had hastened to advise the President:

> Reports contained in the Press indicate that Japan has barred the departure of one hundred American citizens and it is indicated that the detention is in reprisal for the freezing of Japanese assets in the United States of America.
>
> I want to suggest without encroaching upon the privilege of the Executive or without infringing upon the privileges of the State Department that if it is the intention of Japan to enter into a reprisal contest that we remind Nippon that unless assurances are received that Japan will facilitate and permit the voluntary departure of this group of one hundred Americans within forty-eight hours, the Government of the United States will cause the forceful detention or imprisonment in a concentration camp of ten thousand alien Japanese in Hawaii; the ratio of Japanese hostages held by America being one hundred for every American detained by the Mikado's Government.
>
> It would be well to further remind Japan that there are perhaps one hundred fifty thousand additional alien Japanese in the United States who will be held in a reprisal reserve whose status will depend upon Japan's next aggressive move. I feel that the United States is in an ideal position to accept Japan's challenge.
>
> God bless you, Mr. President.[1]

Within two months after the crippling blow dealt by the Japanese at Pearl Harbor, a fast-deteriorating situation in the soon untenable Philippine campaign moved [Secretary of War Henry] Stimson to call for threats of reprisals on Japanese nationals in America "to insure proper treatment" of U.S. citizens trapped in enemy territory. On February 5, the very day when mass evacuation-internment plans began to be drawn up and formalized within the War Department,[2] Stimson wrote [Secretary of State Cordell] Hull:

> General MacArthur has reported in a radiogram, a copy of which is enclosed, that American and British civilians in areas of the Philippines occupied by the Japanese are being subjected to extremely harsh treatment. The unnecessary harsh and rigid measures imposed, in sharp contrast to the moderate treatment of metropolitan Filipinos, are unquestionably designed to discredit the white race.
>
> I request that you strongly protest this unjustified treatment of civilians, and suggest that you present a threat of reprisals against the many Japanese nationals now enjoying negligible restrictions in the United States, to insure proper treatment of our nationals in the Philippines.[3]

If a reprisal reserve urgency had indeed precipitated the sudden decision for internment, the emphasis, as the tide of the war reversed itself, switched to the buildup of a "barter reserve": one sizable enough to allow for the earliest possible repatriation of American detainees, even at the price of a disproportionate number of Japanese nationals in exchange. Behind this willingness on the part of the State Department *to give more than they expected back* may have lurked profound concern that unless meaningful concessions were to be made in the matter of POW exchanges, the whole procedure would get mired in resistance and inertia to the jeopardy of thousands subject to terrible suffering in enemy prison camps.

As revealed in a letter from the Secretary of the Navy to President Roosevelt, the Secretary of State, in Knox's estimate, was being overly disconcerted by the belief that German authorities intended to hold on indefinitely to American detainees "as hostages for captured Germans whom we might prosecute under the war criminal procedure."[4] A similar alarmist concern may have been entertained by Secretary of State Hull as to the intent of Japanese authorities.

The use of the Nisei as part and parcel of this human barter was not totally ruled out in the realm of official thinking. By curious circumstance, such intent on the part of U.S. authorities became starkly evident in the latter part of 1942 and early 1943, when numerous Nisei, to their shocked indignation, were informed by Colonel Karl Bendetsen in a form letter: "Certain Japanese persons are currently being considered for repatriation [expatriation] to Japan. You and those members of your family listed above, are being so considered."[5]

2.

The removals in the United States were only a part of forced uprootings which occurred almost simultaneously in Alaska, Canada, Mexico, Central America, parts of South America, and the Caribbean island of Haiti and the Dominican Republic.

Canada's decision to round up and remove its tiny (23,000) West Coast minority, 75 percent of whom were citizens of Canada, preceded America's by about a month and may have had a decisive influence on the War Department's decision to proceed similarly . . . but, in many ways, discriminatory measures imposed on the Canadian Japanese were more arbitrary and severe. An order of January 14, 1942, calling for the removal of all enemy alien males over sixteen years of age from the area west of the Cascade Mountains resulted in men being separated from women in the initial stage of the evacuation. But a follow-up decree of February 27 demanded total evacuation, citizens as well as aliens, most of whom were removed to work camps and mining "ghost towns" in mountain valleys of the Canadian interior. Property and possessions not disposed of were quickly confiscated and sold off at public auctions since evacuees were expected to assume some of the internment expenses from the proceeds. Canadian Japanese were not permitted to return to British Columbia and their home communities until March 1949, seven years after the evacuation.[6]

Of the 151 Alaskan Japanese plucked from their homes and life pursuits under color of Executive Order 9066, around fifty were seal- and whale-hunting half-Indians and half-Eskimos (*one-half* "Japanese blood" was the criterion in Alaska), some of whom were to associate with Japanese for the first time in the camps. Except for a "few fortunate ones with second-generation fathers,"[7] families were left fatherless since male nationals suffered mass indiscriminate internment in various Justice Department detention centers. Most ended up in the camp maintained exclusively for Japanese alien detainees in Lordsburg, New Mexico. Remaining family members were airlifted to the state of Washington (following a short initial stay at Fort Richardson, Alaska) and penned up temporarily in the Puyallup Assembly Center near Seattle. In the mass Japanese American exodus out of the prohibited military area during the summer of 1942, the evacuees from Alaska wound up in the relocation center of Minidoka in Idaho.

In Mexico, the Japanese residing in small settlements near the American border and coastal areas (along a sixty-two-mile zone) were forced to liquidate their property and move inland, some to "clearing houses" and resettlement camps, a number of them to concentration camps in Perote, Puebla, and Vera Cruz.

Even less selectivity was exercised in the case of the Japanese then scattered throughout the Central American republics. Many were simply "picked up" by reason of their "hostile origin" and handed over to U.S. authorities, who, in turn, arranged for their transportation by sea or air to the U.S. mainland.

Such gunpoint "relocations" to American concentration camps became quite commonplace on the South American continent in the days and months following the Pearl Harbor attack. The reason: Considerable pressure had been applied by the U.S. State Department on various republics of the Western Hemisphere to impound, with the option of handing over to American authorities for care and custody, persons who might be considered "potentially dangerous" to hemispheric security, with special emphasis on the Japanese. More than a month before the war's outbreak, plans for this unusual wartime action began to take shape. On October 20, 1941, U.S. Ambassador to Panama Edwin C. Wilson informed Under Secretary of State Sumner Welles:

> My strictly confidential despatch No. 300 of October 20, 1941, for the Secretary and Under Secretary, transmits memoranda of my conversations with the Foreign Minister regarding the question of internment of Japanese in the event that we suddenly find ourselves at war with Japan.
>
> The attitude of the Panamanian Government is thoroughly cooperative. The final memorandum sets out the points approved by the Panamanian Cabinet for dealing with this matter. Briefly, their thought is this: Immediately following action by the United States to intern Japanese in the United States, Panama would arrest Japanese on Panamanian territory and intern them on Taboga Island. They would be guarded by Panamanian guards and would have the status of Panamanian interns. *All expenses and costs of internment and guarding to be paid by the United States.* The United States Government would agree to hold Panama harmless against any claims which might arise as a result of internment.
>
> I believe it essential that you instruct me by telegraph at once to assure the Foreign Minister that the points which he set out to cover this matter meet the approval of our Government.[8] [Italics mine.]

Funds which would be immediately needed, as in the construction of a prison camp which would serve as a staging area for transshipments to U.S. detention facilities, were to be provided by the Commanding General of the Caribbean Defense Command.[9] And from Chief of Staff General George Marshall came the suggestion that a more liberal interpretation of persons to be detained be considered. On October 28, 1941, he wrote Under Secretary Welles:

> It is gratifying to know that Panama is prepared to intern Japanese aliens immediately following similar action by the United States.

I suggest, however, that the agreement be enlarged to provide for internment by the Panamanian Government of all persons believed dangerous, who are regarded by the United States as enemy aliens, under similar conditions.[10]

Similarly encouraged to undermine in advance any possibility of Japanese sabotage, subversion, or fifth-column treachery was Panama's neighbor republic of Costa Rica. On December 8, 1941, upon America's declaration of war on Japan, the U.S. Legation in Costa Rica wired the State Department: . . . ORDERS FOR INTERNMENT OF ALL JAPANESE IN COSTA RICA HAVE BEEN ISSUED.[11]

At a Conference of Foreign Ministers of the American Republics held in Rio de Janeiro in January 1942, a special inter-American agency (the Emergency Committee for Political Defense) to coordinate hemispheric security measures was organized, with headquarters subsequently established in Montevideo. The Emergency Committee adopted, without delay, a resolution which had been drafted by the U.S. Department of Justice in conjunction with the Department of State which stressed the need for prompt preventive detention of dangerous Axis nationals and for the "deportation of such persons to another American republic for detention when adequate local detention facilities are lacking."[12] States interested in the collaborative effort were assured that not only detention accommodations but also shipping facilities would be provided by the United States "at its own expense."[13] The State Department offered an additional incentive: It would include any of the official and civilian nationals of the participating republics in whatever exchange arrangements the U.S. would subsequently make with Axis powers.

More than a dozen American states cooperated. Among them: Bolivia, Colombia, Costa Rica, the Dominican Republic, Ecuador, El Salvador, Guatemala, Haiti, Honduras, Mexico, Nicaragua, Panama, Peru, and Venezuela.[14] Three states, Brazil, Uruguay, and Paraguay, instituted their own detention programs (Paraguay, for one, promptly arrested the two Japanese residing within her borders). Since Argentina and Chile held back breaking off diplomatic relations with the Axis powers until much later, both nations took no part in the hemispheric imprisonments.

In time, the State Department was able to claim that "the belligerent republics of the Caribbean area have sent us subversive aliens without limitation concerning their disposition"; but four republics—Venezuela, Colombia, Ecuador, and Mexico—exacted "explicit guarantees" before turning over internees.[15] Panama liberally granted the U.S. "full freedom to negotiate with Japan and agrees to the use of Japanese internees . . . for exchange of any non-official citizen of an American belligerent country."[16]

The concept of hemispheric removals had its origin in the State Department, but responsibility for the success of the operation was shared by the Departments of War, Navy, and Justice.[17] With the safety of the Panama Canal a veritable life-or-death matter after the near annihilation of the Pacific Fleet, it appears that all concerned acted on the conviction that the threat to continental security was so grave as to outweigh the momentary misuse of executive, military, and judicial power.

As a direct result of the hemispheric nations' agreement to "cooperate jointly for their mutual protection," over two thousand deportees of Japanese ancestry were to swell the already impressive U.S. barter reserve by ending up in scattered mainland detention camps, whose existence was virtually unknown then to the American public. . . . Though the deportees were legally in State Department custody, the custodial program for them was supervised by the Immigration and Naturalization Service of the U.S. Justice Department.

3.

As for persons of Japanese ancestry residing in the democratic republic of Peru, racial antagonism fed by resentment of the foreign element as being exceedingly successful economic competitors had more to do with the Peruvian Government's spirited cooperation than its concern for the defense of the Hemisphere. The steady economic encroachment of the resident Japanese and their alleged imperviousness to assimilation had aroused increasing nativist hostility; and anti-Japanese legislation and restrictive ordinances of the West Coast type had been copied through the years, culminating with the revocation, by executive action, of citizenship rights of Nisei possessing dual citizenship. Racial feelings against the Japanese minority, abetted by the press, had burst into occasional mob action even before the Pearl Harbor attack. And much of the blame for the cut-off of Japanese immigration in 1936 had been attributed to the "social unrest" stirred up by the unwanted minority because, in the words of Foreign Minister Ulloa, "their conditions and methods of working have produced pernicious competition for the Peruvian workers and businessmen."

Accordingly, 80 percent of the Latin-American deportees of Japanese ancestry was to be contributed by the government of Peru, an enthusiasm stimulated not only by the opportunity presented to expropriate property and business (Law No. 9586 of April 10 authorized seizure of Axis property) but also to rid the realm of an undesirable element. On July 20, 1942, Henry Norweb, the U.S. Ambassador to Peru, informed the State Department of President Manuel Prado's manifest fervor in this regard:

The second matter in which the President [Prado] is very much interested is the possibility of getting rid of the Japanese in Peru. He would like to settle this problem permanently, which means that he is thinking in terms of repatriating thousands of Japanese. He asked Colonel Lord to let him know about the prospects of additional shipping facilities from the United States. In any arrangement that might be made for internment of Japanese in the States, Peru would like to be sure that these Japanese would not be returned to Peru later on. The President's goal apparently is the substantial elimination of the Japanese colony in Peru.[18]

Pressure in the name of "mutual protection" had obviously paid off. Only three months earlier, a dispatch from the American Embassy in Lima had underscored the gravity of the subversion potential inherent in the Peruvian Japanese, "whose strength and ability have, in the past, been vastly underestimated and whose fanatic spirit has neither been understood nor taken seriously. . . . there appears to be little realization of the actual danger and a reluctance on the part of the Government to take positive measures." Recommendations from the Legation included the removal of key Japanese leaders, the encouragement of "propaganda intended to call attention of the Peruvians to the Japanese dangers," and suggestion that covert assistance might even be rendered by U.S. authorities: "Ways may be found to provide . . . material without of course permitting the source to become known as the Embassy."[19]

In light of such concerns among Embassy officials of the Lima Legation, the Peruvian President's unexpected eagerness to cooperate to the fullest came as a welcome turn of events and as an instant go-ahead for the core of U.S. advisers to assist in widening the scope of Peruvian expulsions. An intradepartmental State Department memo noted ways in which the operation might be expedited:

President Prado has officially stated his willingness to have this deportation program carried through. . . . The suggestion that Japanese be removed from strategic areas should be followed and this should be carried on by *well-paid* police; even if this necessitates a loan from this government. All police charged with supervision of Japanese should be well paid. [Legation had warned that Peruvian law officers "are susceptible to Japanese bribes . . . their alertness cannot be depended upon."] The suggestion that Japanese be expelled whether they are naturalized Peruvians or not might be met by a denaturalization law.[20]

Arrests were made in swift, silent raids by the Peruvian police, who first confined detainees in local jails, then turned them over to the custody of U.S. military authorities. Then began the strange odyssey which would take them northward to the United States mainland: "We were taken to the port of Callao and embarked on an American transport under strict guard and with machine gun pointed at us by American soldiers."[21] As it was found that immunity from deportation could be "bought" by a generous bribe unless the removal was swiftly expedited, Army Air Transport planes were used in a number of cases involving the "extremely dangerous," usually the wealthier and influential Peruvian Japanese considered high-priority trade bait. After a short stopover in the Panama-based internment camp used as a staging area, deportees were shipped on to various Department of Justice detention centers in the States, after landing at a Gulf Coast or West Coast port.

More fortunate prisoners enjoyed reunion with family members at the Crystal City Internment Camp in Texas, the only "family camp" operated by the Justice Department where detainees were dealt with as "prisoners of war." Even the voluntary prisoners. The latter were mostly women and children. A total of 1,094 of them, officially designated as "voluntary detainees," answered the State Department's "invitation" to place themselves in war-duration voluntary incarceration with the 1,024 men who had been seized and spirited to the mainland by the U.S. military.

The question of whether the reunion program had been undertaken as a direct means of swelling the U.S. barter stockpile or whether the entire procedure represented a "humanitarian" concession on the part of the State and Justice departments is a matter still shrouded in mystery.[22]

By late October of 1942, fears concerning hemispheric security had greatly diminished. A pounding U.S. counteroffensive in the Solomons had finally begun to check the thrust of the Japanese juggernaut in the Pacific. And with the mass transportation of the coastal subnation to the inland camps nearing completion, Hull hastened to advise the President of what, to the Secretary of State, were still overriding reasons why there should be no letup in the hemispheric removal — at least of "all the Japanese . . . for internment in the United States."

There are in China 3,300 American citizens who desire to return to the United States. Many of them are substantial persons who have represented important American business and commercial interests and a large number of missionaries. They are scattered all through that part of China occupied by the Japanese. Some of them are at liberty, some of them are in concentration camps, and some of them have limited liberty, but all of them subject to momentary cruel and harsh treatment by their oppressors. Under our agreement with Japan which is still operating, we will be able to remove these people. It will take two more trips of the *Gripsholm** to do so. In exchange for them we will have to send out Japanese in the same quantity. . . .

Gripsholm: a Swedish motor ship that transported people of Japanese ancestry from the United States to Japan during the war.

In addition, there are 3,000 non-resident American citizens in the Philippines. We have no agreement for their exchange but it has been intimated that Japan might consider an exchange of them. It would be very gratifying if we could obtain those people from Japanese control and return them to the United States. But to do so we would have to exchange Japanese for them. That would take two more round trips of the *Gripsholm.*

Still, in addition, there are 700 civilians interned in Japan proper captured at Guam and Wake. It is probable that we might arrange for their return. But in order to obtain them we would have to release Japanese. . . .

With the foregoing as a predicate, I propose the following course of action:

. . . Continue our exchange agreement with the Japanese until the Americans are out of China, Japan and the Philippines — so far as possible. . . .

Continue our efforts to remove all the Japanese from these American Republic countries for internment in the United States.

Continue our efforts to remove from South and Central America all the dangerous Germans and Italians still there, together with their families. . . .[23]

[Reparagraphed by author of this selection]

In the Secretary of State's recommended course of action, the precise wording of the directive is significant: Note the qualifying prerequisite, *dangerous,* in reference to hostages-to-be of German and Italian nationalities. In Hull's implied suggestion of more discriminating treatment of non-Oriental Axis nationals, while calling for wholesale removal — dangerous or harmless — of "all the Japanese," evidence again lies tellingly exposed of racial bias then lurking in high and rarefied places in the nation's capital.

4.

By early 1943, the Justice Department, in its custodial role in the hemispheric operation, had become greatly alarmed at the number of internees being sent up. Worse, it had come to its attention that many being held under the Alien Enemies Act were not enemy Japanese but Peruvian nationals, thus aliens of a friendly nation; and that little or no evidence supported the Peruvian Government's contention that their deportees were dangerous. "Some of the cases seem to be mistakes," Attorney General Biddle wrote the Secretary of State on January 11, 1943.[24]

Biddle insisted on more conclusive proof that the deportees were in fact "the dangerous leaders among the Japanese population in Peru," and he proposed sending his own representative to Peru and other donor nations to help sort out the people to be sent up. Since barter negotiations between Washington and Tokyo had then come to a standstill, Biddle balked at going along with the indiscriminate internment of bodies being sent up in ever-growing numbers from Peru, insisting that his department had merely agreed to "expediting *temporary* custody" pending repatriation.

The State Department's primary concern was that the competence and sincerity of the donor states would be impugned if Biddle were to challenge the veracity of their criterion of "dangerousness." But the State Department finally gave in, and Raymond W. Ickes (of the Central and South American division of the Alien Enemy Control unit) of the Justice Department was permitted to make on-the-spot reviews of all pending deportee cases. Ickes found little evidence anywhere to support the claims of the participating republics that individuals being held — or targeted — for deportation were "in any true sense of the word security subjects." On turning down the deportation from Venezuela of thirty Japanese, he advised the U.S. Legation in Caracas:

> This is the very thing that we have to guard against, particularly in the case of Peru, where attempts have been made to send job lots of Japanese to the States merely because the Peruvians wanted their businesses and not because there was any adverse evidence against them.[25]

All deportations to the United States thereafter ceased.

With the coming of peace, the once felicitous relationship between the U.S. and Peru suffered another setback. While the State Department proceeded to return various ex-hostages to their respective homelands, the government of Peru refused to allow reentry in the case of Japanese. Only a few select citizens were permitted readmission, mostly native-Peruvian wives and Peruvian-citizen children.

The Justice Department thereupon pressed ahead with an extraordinary piece of injustice on the onetime kidnapees no longer needed to ransom off U.S. detainees. With certain hierarchal changes in the Department (FDR's death on April 12, 1945, had resulted in Tom Clark, a Truman appointee, becoming Attorney General on September 27, 1945), all were scheduled for removal to Japan despite vigorous protest that a sizable number of them had no ties in a country many had never visited; wives and children of many were in fact still living in Peru.[26] The grounds for the second "deportation" of the Peruvian kidnapees was that they lacked proper credentials: they had entered the U.S. illegally, without visas and without passports.[27]

From despair arising from their prolonged detention without the possibility of return to their homeland or release, a contingent of some 1,700 Peruvian Japanese (700 men and their dependents) allowed themselves, between November 1945 and February 1946,[28] to be "voluntarily" unloaded on Japan. Many had acquiesced to this drastic federal action in the belief that reunion with families left behind in Peru could not otherwise be achieved.

Awaiting a similarly grim fate were 365 remaining Peruvian rejects, whose desperate plight came to the attention of Wayne Collins, a San Francisco attorney then conducting a one-man war against the Justice Department in trying to extricate thousands of Nisei caught in their "renunciation trap" . . . , another one of the extreme consequences of the evacuation tragedy.

To abort U.S. plans to "dump" this residual Peruvian group on a defeated, war-pulverized enemy hardly able to care for its own starving masses, Collins filed two test proceedings in habeas corpus on June 25, 1946, in a U.S. District Court in San Francisco after the Immigration Department contended that suspension of deportation on a like basis as Caucasians was not permitted, and a subsequent appeal directly to the Attorney General and the President came to no avail.[29] With the removal program brought, by court action, to a forced halt, the detainees were placed in "relaxed internment"— many of them at Seabrook Farms, New Jersey, the well-known frozen food processing plant where the labor of German POWs had been utilized during the war years, and where evacuee groups from many camps were given employment.

Collins, with the aid of the Northern California office of the American Civil Liberties Union, also sought to bring to public attention what both contended was a "legalized kidnaping" program masterminded by the State Department and sanctioned by the nation's chief guardian of decency and legality, the Attorney General, whose office and the State Department now disclaimed any responsibility for the plight of the unfortunate people.

Interior Secretary Harold Ickes (father of Raymond W. Ickes), the only high-level officer of the FDR Administration to speak out in criticism of the State and Justice departments' highly clandestine proceedings, took issue with Attorney General Clark, then seeking the U.S. Vice-Presidency spot by paying glowing homage to the nation's democratic ideals of human rights and individual liberty. This did not sit well with former Cabinet officer Ickes, who knew, through and through, the wartime injustices perpetrated on the Issei and Nisei throughout the Western Hemisphere, which, even then, were being perpetuated by Attorney General Clark's zealous pursuance of postwar deportations of "disloyals" and scores of defenseless aliens under arbitrary classification as "dangerous."[30]

Ickes was sharply outspoken:

> What the country demands from the Attorney General is less self-serving lip-service and more action. . . .
>
>   The Attorney General, in the fashion of the Russian Secret Police, maintains a top-secret list of individuals and organizations supposed to be subversive or disloyal. What are the criteria for judging whether a person is disloyal? . . .

I cannot begin . . . even to call the role of our maimed, mutilated, and miss-
ing civil liberties, but the United States, more than two years after the war, is
holding in internment some 293 naturalized Peruvians of Japanese descent,
who were taken by force by our State and Justice Departments from their
homes in Peru.[31]

The resolution of the Peruvian-Japanese dilemma was to take years of
unprecedented legal maneuvering on the part of lawyer Collins to untangle
the mess in which so many charged with not one specifiable offense found
themselves — their lives often mangled beyond repair through the prolonged splitting of families.

Changes in U.S. laws eventually enabled the Peruvian Japanese to apply
for suspension of deportation if it could be shown that deportation to Japan
would result in serious economic hardship and if "continued residence" in
the United States of at least ten years could be proved — with years spent in
various concentration camps counting also as "residence."

Peru finally permitted reentry of the deportees in the mid-1950s, but less
than one hundred returned. By then the job of reconstructing their lives
had begun elsewhere.

Three hundred of the 365 rescued by Collins chose to remain in the
United States. An impressive number became American citizens under the
amended U.S. naturalization law of 1952, which finally gave immigrants of
Asian ancestry the right to become Americans.[32]

Notes

1. Letter, John D. Dingell to Roosevelt, August 18, 1941, OF 197, FDR Library.
Dingell was grossly mistaken in claiming that there were 150,000 "additional alien
Japanese in the United States." The 1940 census shows 126,947 Japanese Americans
in the continental U.S., *only 47,305 of them aliens.* Two-thirds of the minority (79,642)
were native-born U.S. citizens.

2. Three rough drafts (all dated "2/5/42") recommending "steps to be taken in
connection with the alien enemy-potential saboteur" problem provide evidence of
being precursors to the document, Executive Order 9066, which would authorize
the West Coast and other mass evacuations on U.S. soil. An early draft reads: "Initially, exclusions to be essentially by class, viz. on the Pacific Coast all Japanese (except, perhaps, for a few token Japs to sustain the legality)." The drafts' opening
sentences vary somewhat: (1) "Colonel Bendetsen recommends . . ."; (2) "I recommend . . ."; (3) "The War Department recommends . . .". Unnumbered documents from records of the Office of Assistant Secretary of War, RG 107, National Archives. See also pp. 69, 94, and 95.

3. Letter, Henry L. Stimson to Cordell Hull, February 5, 1942, Department of
State File 740.00115 Pacific War/153, RG 59, National Archives.

4. Letter, Frank Knox to Roosevelt, August 16, 1943, PSF: War Department, FDR
Library. Hull had asked for the go-ahead which would have authorized repatriation

of 266 U.S. citizens in return for approximately 750 German nationals being held in the U.S.

5. Wartime Civil Control Administration Form R-104. The State Department's Repatriation Section of the Special War Problems Division maintained a list of 100,000 names of "individuals of the Japanese race in the United States" along with "their correct addresses, and with the necessary information concerning their identification, whereabouts, and repatriability" (*Department of State Bulletin*, August 6, 1944, p. 142). Tokyo was explicit as to persons to be exchanged, therefore much misunderstanding resulted among detainees from the department's desire to fulfill the Japanese Government's "priority list."

6. "New Day for Nisei Canadians," *Pacific Citizen*, February 12, 1949. Canada had refused to induct the Nisei during wartime, and only in 1947 were citizens of Japanese descent given the right to vote. . . .

7. Letter, M.H. to Hon. Ernest Gruening, October 20, 1942, RG 210, National Archives, in which a Nisei youth implores Governor Gruening of Alaska to help alleviate the plight of the Alaskan Nisei separated from fathers: "You no doubt already know that there are more than 120 Alaskans in this camp. . . . Of this number about 50 are children under the age of 18 years. The problem arises from the fact that the Alaskan children . . . are without their paternal guidance. Not a single normal family head is with his respective families."

8. Letter, Edwin C. Wilson to Sumner Welles, October 20, 1941, Department of State File 740.00115 Pacific War/1 1/3, RG 59, National Archives.

9. Wire, Cordell Hull to Ambassador (Wilson), December 12, 1941, Department of State File 740.00115 Pacific War/6, RG 59, National Archives. The U.S. Ambassador to Panama was instructed by Hull to see that the Commanding General "furnish the necessary military guard and medical services until such time as the Panamanian officials assume full control of the camp."

10. Letter, George Marshall to Sumner Welles, October 28, 1941, Department of State File 740.00115 Pacific War/1 2/3, RG 59, National Archives.

11. Telegram #375, Arthur Bliss Lane to State Department, December 8, 1941, Department of State File 740.00115 Pacific War/9, RG 59, National Archives.

12. *Department of State Building*, August 6, 1944, p. 146. The Emergency Committee for Political Defense served to augment removal pressure being applied by the State Department. "It is hoped that pressure from this Committee . . . may increase the effectiveness of Mexican cooperation in the relatively near future," stated a dispatch to Cordell Hull which criticized the government's "apathy." Memorandum, Harold D. Finley (First Secretary to Embassy) to the Secretary of State, January 19, 1942, Department of State File 740.00115 Pacific War/53, RG 59, National Archives.

13. Ibid., p. 147. The Special War Problems Division of the Department of State handled all shipping arrangements. In most instances, Army transports were utilized to bring up detainees.

14. See Edward N. Barnhart's "Japanese Internees from Peru," *Pacific Historical Review*, Vol. 31, May 1962, p. 172, fn. 13. Though not mentioned by Barnhart, Mexico and Venezuela were also participants. Barnhart claims that, in all, "over 600 German nationals and a few men of Italian and other nationality" were also removed to U.S. detention facilities from these countries.

15. *Department of State Bulletin*, op. cit., p. 147. Alien deportees were still considered to be under the "jurisdiction" of the donor state, which meant that prior approval was required as to the disposition of each case.

16. Wire, Ambassador Wilson to Secretary of State, May 16, 1942, Department of State File 740.00115 Pacific War/548, RG 59, National Archives. . . .

17. *Department of State Bulletin,* op. cit., p. 146. The legislative branch of the government was apparently kept in the dark. As for the President, Warren Page Rucker in his well-documented unpublished M.A. thesis ("United States–Peruvian Policy toward Peruvian-Japanese Persons during World War II," University of Virginia, 1970) maintains: ". . . there seems little doubt . . . that he [FDR] was aware of the internment of the Peruvian-Japanese and that it met with his approval."

18. Letter, Henry Norweb to Sumner Welles, July 20, 1942, Department of State File 740.00115 Pacific War/1002 2/6, RG 59, National Archives. The Japanese colony in Peru was then estimated to number between 25,000 and 30,000.

10. Taken from Enclosure 1 (Memorandum to Ambassador Norweb from John K. Emmerson, Third Secretary of Embassy, April 18, 1942) to dispatch No. 3422 to State Department, April 21, 1942, Department of State File 894.20223/124, RG 59, National Archives. Norweb, in the accompanying dispatch to Hull, endorsed the recommendations as "sound and well presented."

20. Memorandum, Philip W. Bonsal to Selden Chapin, September 26, 1942, Department of State File 740.00115 Pacific War/1002 5/6, RG 59, National Archives.

21. Letter, V.K.T. to Spanish Ambassador, June 30, 1944, unnumbered document from Department of State File, RG 59, National Archives. Charges of abusive treatment were filed by a number of deportees over the years. . . .

22. Tokyo protests had stressed the inhumanity of the removals, which left families "abandoned and without resources." There is reason to believe that, as a direct result of Tokyo threats of "adequate counter measures," the family reunion program had been instituted. Tokyo was subsequently informed that initially "the facilities used for the transportation . . . were not adapted to the transportation of women and children" but that the U.S. intended to bring them over "at the earliest practicable opportunity." Memorandum, State Department to Spanish Embassy, April 19, 1943, Department of State File 740.00115 Pacific War/1549, RG 59, National Archives. Interestingly, commercial airlines and steamship lines were used in the transport of family members. . . .

23. Letter, Cordell Hull to Roosevelt, August 27, 1942, OF 20, FDR Library. At the time, mail, medicine, and other relief supplies could be sent to civilians and American POWs in Japanese hands only by way of the exchange vessels.

24. Letter, Francis Biddle to Secretary of State, January 11, 1943, Department of State File 740.00115 Pacific War/1276, RG 59, National Archives. The Alien Enemies Act (of 1798) provides that whenever there is a declared war between the U.S. and any foreign nation, "all natives, citizens, denizens, or subjects of the hostile nation," fourteen years or older, can be "apprehended, restrained, secured, and removed as alien enemies."

25. As quoted in a memorandum to the Secretary of State from Frank P. Corrigan of the U.S. Embassy in Caracas, August 21, 1943, Department of State File 740.00115 Pacific War/1845, RG 59, National Archives.

26. The drastic U.S. removal policy gained impetus from a resolution adopted at an Inter-American Conference in the spring of 1945. The resolution had recommended the adoption of measures "to prevent any person whose deportation was necessary for reasons of security of the continent from further residing in this hemisphere, if such residence would be prejudicial to the future security or welfare of the Americas." A Presidential Proclamation (Truman) of September 8, 1945, imple-

mented the resolution by directing the Justice Department to assist the Secretary of State (Byrnes) in effectuating removal of all enemy aliens to lands belonging to the enemy governments "to which or to the principles of which they had adhered" and of others then in the U.S. "without admission under the immigration laws." See Department of State File 711.62115 AR/8-3145, RG 59, National Archives.

27. The impossibility of a case-by-case review may also have led to the decision for summary removals. According to a State Department memo: ". . . unless we can get Peru to take the Japanese back, we shall be forced to repatriate all of them to Japan, since we have no information which would enable us to make a case-by-case review. In the very great majority of the cases, the Japanese were sent here only on the say-so of the Peruvian Government." Memorandum, J. B. Bingham to Braden and Acheson, December 13, 1945, Department of State File FW 711.62115 AR/12-1345, RG 59, National Archives.

28. Alfred Steinberg, "'Blunder' Maroons Peruvian Japanese in the U.S.," *Washington Post,* September 26, 1948. Author Barnhart ("Japanese Internees from Peru") maintains that the group removed during this period totaled 1,700, which is at variance with the State Department claim of 1,440 who "voluntarily returned to Japan." Letter to author from Georgia D. Hill, Office of the Chief of Military History, December 19, 1972. There had been 476 Peruvian-Japanese included in the second exchange of prisoners with Japan (September, 1943). See "Japanese in Peru" by John K. Emmerson, October 9, 1943, Department of State File 894.20223/196, National Archives.

29. Memorandum, Wayne Collins to author, postmarked June 28, 1973. Aliens among the residual group of 365 had been informed on March 26, 1946: ". . . deportation proceedings are to be instituted immediately in the cases of all who do not file applications for voluntary repatriation. Require all to make their intentions known within twenty-four hours." (Wire to officer in charge of Crystal City from the Immigration and Naturalization Service, excerpted from the Rucker study.) Collins maintains that the earlier removal of 1,700 deportees had been in no way voluntary "even if each was asked and signified his or her desire to be transported to Japan. They were being held as alien enemies under the Alien Enemies Act and couldn't escape the internment unless they agreed to be sent to Japan. That is a perfect picture of duress and lacks every essential of voluntariness."

30. Ickes wrote in his *New York Post* column (as reported in the *Pacific Citizen,* June 29, 1946) that the record of Japanese aliens in the United States during the war as "loyal Americans" is "unblemished," and that "the immediate problem is one of halting the brutal deportation of alien Japanese who have suffered so much at the hands of 'free and democratic' America." Collins successfully halted deportation of 163 longtime residents of fine standing found to be illegal entrants and of numerous Japanese nationals who had lost their admission status as a result of the war.

31. "Town Meeting of the Air" broadcast of December 2, 1947, in *The Town Hall,* XIII, No. 32 (December 12, 1947).

32. The deportees became eligible for naturalization under Public Law 751 (68 Stat., 1044), of August 31, 1954, which entitled the Peruvian-Japanese to a certification of "authorized entry" into the United States (Barnhart, op. cit., p. 176). The Peruvian-Japanese were "specifically denied restitution for damages by a House bill [H.R. 3999 *Adjudication of Certain Claims of Persons of Japanese Ancestry,* 80th Congress, 1st sess.] passed in July of 1947." (Rucker, op. cit., p. 65.)

Gary Y. Okihiro

Tule Lake under Martial Law: A Study in Japanese Resistance

Whereas the selections by Roger Daniels, Peter Irons, and Michi Weglyn analyze the motives and policies of government officials, recent scholarship has focused on Japanese American responses to mass incarceration. The author of this selection, Gary Okihiro, was one of the first revisionist historians to reinterpret protest within the internment camps. Born in 1945, Okihiro grew up in Hawaii far away from the Tule Lake Segregation Center in California. But Okihiro decided to research the protests at Tule Lake because, like many historians of the 1970s, he was fascinated by the topic of resistance. Influenced by the social movements of the 1960s, these revisionist scholars began writing histories of people of color challenging racial oppression in America and the rest of the world.

Okihiro first studied African resistance to colonization. His service in the Peace Corps, in Botswana in 1968, convinced him of the need to "decolonize the writing of the past" by restoring the voices and experiences of Africans to history. In 1976, he received a Ph.D. in history from the University of California at Los Angeles after completing his dissertation, "Hunters, Herders, Cultivators, and Traders: Interaction and Change in the Kgalagadi, Nineteenth Century." As a graduate student, he also helped develop Asian American studies at UCLA and began exploring the history of internment. In 1972, he made a pilgrimage to the remains of what had been the Manzanar camp, 225 miles north of Los Angeles. In the book *Whispered Silences: Japanese Americans and*

World War II (1996), he later recalled the profound impact of this journey:

> I discovered a great truth that Manzanar spring day, when surrounded by the silences of the snow-flecked mountains, the barren desert sand, and the stone and concrete foundations; I found a quickening in the wasteland, a scent in the wind. The burial ground was overfull with life. The silences of the past, I discovered, were not empty of meaning. Our stories, if missing from the pages of history, advance other stories, other lives.[1]

Inspired to restore internees to the pages of history, Okihiro reexamined the camp records produced by the War Relocation Authority (WRA) and the Japanese American Evacuation and Resettlement Study (JERS). This research made him determined to destroy the "myth of the loyal and subject victim" promoted by earlier accounts. In the pioneering article "Japanese Resistance in America's Concentration Camps: A Re-evaluation" (1973), Okihiro urged Asian American scholars to apply the insights provided in books such as Herbert Aptheker's *American Slave Revolts* (1963) and Nicholas Halasz's *The Rattling Chains* (1966). The history of noncooperation and mass demonstrations at the Poston and Manzanar camps, he argued, demonstrated that Japanese Americans also had a vital and resilient tradition of resisting oppression.

Tule Lake, as this selection shows, provided fertile ground for a revisionist interpretation of resistance. Located in northern California, just south of the Oregon border, the camp had a turbulent history even before it became a segregation center. In August 1942, two and a half months after the camp opened, farm laborers went on strike over the lack of promised goods and salaries. Packing shed workers struck the next month, and mess hall workers staged a protest in October. Administrative blunders and a strong dissident leadership exacerbated anger at the entire "leave clearance" process, and one-third of the camp refused to register or sign the loyalty questionnaire in February 1943. The WRA then converted Tule Lake into a segregation center for those deemed disloyal in all the camps. Protests escalated, and in early November the army took over and declared martial law. Military rule, as the following selection shows, only inspired more demonstrations and resistance.

In the 1970s, few academic journals were willing to publish Okihiro's revisionist interpretations because the editors didn't consider Japanese American protests a part of American history or Western history. Okihiro found receptive editors at the newly established *Amerasia Journal* and the *Journal of Ethnic Studies*. In the mid-1970s, he abandoned his plans to write a book on Tule Lake after failing to find any interested publishers. In the 1980s and 1990s, however, ethnic studies flourished, and Okihiro was recognized as a leading scholar in the field. He edited an anthology on African, Caribbean, and African American resistance and cowrote a book on Japanese American farmers in California's Santa Clara Valley. In *Cane Fires: The Anti-Japanese Movement in Hawaii, 1865–1945* (1991), Okihiro contests the popular image of the islands as a "racial paradise." The book also drew attention to the suffering of islanders arrested by the FBI and interned in camps run by the Army and the Department of Justice during World War II. Long neglected because of the focus on WRA camps, these internees also appear in Okihiro's text accompanying Joan Myers's photographs of the remnants of the internment camps in *Whispered Silences: Japanese Americans and World War II* (1996).

After nurturing Asian American studies programs at Humboldt State University and Santa Clara University, Okihiro joined the Cornell University history department in 1989. Currently the director of the Asian American Studies Program at Cornell, he also has served as president of the Association of Asian American Studies and is editor of the *Journal of Asian American Studies*. He continues to assail "traditional" views of history, most recently in his book *Margins and Mainstreams: Asians in American History and Culture* (1994), where he says that the democratic "core values and ideals of the nation" emanate from the struggles for equality by "Asian and African Americans, Latinos and American Indians, women, and gays and lesbians."[2]

Questions for a Closer Reading

1. Okihiro criticizes the "didactic approach" of earlier internment studies that focus on moral lessons and theories of responsibility. Why does he call for a new perspective on internment? How does his research help him undermine the "myth of the model minority"?

2. How does Okihiro challenge orthodox interpretations of resistance in the camps? Do you find his reinterpretation of the causes and consequences of camp protest persuasive?

3. Okihiro describes a spectrum of protest at Tule Lake. How does he explain the differences between "the more conservative protesters who hoped for a post-war future in America" and the most militant protesters?

4. What impact did military rule have on the influence of the *Daihyo Sha Kai*? Why, according to Okihiro, did the camp split over maintaining the status quo?

5. After noting differences between groups of resisters, Okihiro maintains that, "in the final analysis," they were "united in the underlying and pervasive struggle for human rights." Do you agree with Okihiro's argument that there was no "dramatic break" in the history of resistance at Tule Lake? Why or why not?

Notes

1. *Whispered Silences: Japanese Americans and World War II,* essay by Gary Y. Okihiro, photographs by Joan Myers (Seattle: University of Washington Press, 1996), p. 241.

2. Gary Y. Okihiro, "Preface," *Margins and Mainstreams: Asians in American History* (Seattle: University of Washington Press, 1994), p. ix.

Tule Lake under Martial Law:
A Study in Japanese Resistance

The wartime internment of persons of Japanese ancestry has drawn considerable attention primarily because it serves the purposes of writers whose concerns are wider than the historical experience itself. There are those who regard the internment experience as historically significant because of its instructional value. That didactic approach, which forms a basis for the orthodox interpretation of the camps, has been the hallmark of popular writers, journalists, civil rights activists, ex–War Relocation Authority (WRA) officials, and members of the Japanese American Citizens League (JACL). To them, the forced removal and internment of 110,000 persons of Japanese ancestry was America's greatest wartime mistake, and the episode is a moral lesson to the nation, teaching that constant vigilance must be maintained to safeguard the civil liberties of all citizens because it could happen again to any minority group. Accordingly, those authors display a preoccupation with theories of responsibility for the mass removal and internment, and with constitutional issues.[1]

Apart from those concerns, the authors of the orthodox interpretation wrote with polemical objects in mind. While there were a few ex–WRA administrators who had an interest in answering their critics' charge of maladministration, the basic thrust of the authors of the orthodoxy was to refute the justification that "a Jap is a Jap." Their argument was based on the findings of sociologists who studied the camp communities and observed that Japanese society was not monolithic but was composed of what they determined to be geo-generational cleavages and varying degrees of assimilation. That refinement, when combined with other factors such as the education of Kibei* in Japan, formed the basis for their explanation for

---

Kibei: a term for Japanese Americans born in the United States but sent to Japan for their education.

Gary Y. Okihiro, "Tule Lake under Martial Law: A Study in Japanese Resistance," *Journal of Ethnic Studies* 5, no. 3 (Fall 1977): 71–85.

resistance in the internment camps. Their conclusion was that not all Japanese were the same, and that although there were some who were "pro-Japan" in sentiment, the vast majority were loyal to America. While that insight was an advance over the racists' indiscriminate stereotype, it simply replaced one stereotype with another. Issei were generally seen as "pro-Japan" in sentiment, Kibei were simplistically equated with "troublemakers," and Nisei, as assimilated and "pro-American."[2]

Another stereotype and myth was that the Japanese surmounted the overwhelming odds of early White racism, confiscation of property, and internment to become America's model minority. The story of the Japanese in America, therefore, is a stirring chapter in American history in which an entire ethnic minority showed America to be a land of opportunity and of justice triumphant.[3] The internment experience is crucial to that myth of the model minority. By demonstrating the innocence of the Japanese, their forbearance and fortitude throughout internment, and their unswerving pro-American loyalty despite being deprived of their rights as citizens, the cornerstone of the myth is laid. From the fires of adversity came a people ennobled. Therefore, the visible forms of Japanese resistance in the internment camps must be explained in terms other than resistance against White racism and anti-Americanism.

The orthodox interpretation explains Japanese resistance in the internment camps by citing the inexperience of the WRA administrators and the novelty of the situation. Once those initial problems had been resolved, that explanation concludes, resistance disappeared.[4] The frustration-aggression theory underlies a second explanation for the causes of Japanese resistance in the camps. This explanation views the various forms of resistance, the strike or "riot," as expressions and releases of pent-up pressures and frustrations.[5] A third causal explanation portrays resistance as an internal geo-generational struggle between Issei and Nisei, and Japanese from California set against those from the Pacific Northwest.[6] And finally, a fourth explanation admits to the presence of pro-Axis sympathizers among the internees, notably the Kibei, but it claims that these were only a small minority within the community. According to this explanation, Japanese resistance was generated by these troublemakers who stirred up discontent and used bullying tactics to coerce others to join in their protest.[7]

A small, but growing body of writings has questioned in recent years the orthodox interpretation of the internment camp.[8] These revisionists point out that the wartime removal of Japanese cannot be removed from its pre-war historical context and that the internment camps were a logical extension of the established pattern of interaction between White Americans and Yellow immigrants.[9] Further, Japanese resistance in the camps was a part of that historical legacy, its roots reaching back in time to the daily struggle for survival in a racist American West; it was continuous, and purposeful. The revisionists view the camps and Japanese resistance from the perspective of historical continuities and linkages, and they deny the orthodox interpretation of treating resistance in terms of unconnected "incidents," minority "troublemakers" and "pressure groups," and geo-generational cleavages. And finally, instead of using the internment camps to illustrate a point external to that experience as do writers of the orthodoxy, the revisionists stress that the experience is not so much a moral lesson to White America as it is a part of the history of Asians in America.

There are a number of difficulties in the revisionists' interpretation of the internment camps. A major impediment is the nature of the available sources. Early analysts of the camps all wrote from the orthodox point of view and the resource materials assembled as documents, letters, memoirs, and oral history tapes all reflect the biases of the WRA and the JACL. Until a more comprehensive and objective collection of reminiscences can be made of those who formed the camp majority, we will regrettably be limited by those myopic confines. Because of that barrier, the revisionists are unable to determine precisely the number of people who actually resisted, the degree of mobilization, the exact role of coercion, and even the forms and nature of resistance. In addition, there is a notable gap in their attempt to link resistance in the camps with Japanese resistance to white racism in pre-war America. At this stage, it is too early to speak with any degree of certainty, and the revisionists can only legitimately claim that their interpretation represents a more reasonable attempt than the orthodox view. What is needed are a number of micro-studies which demonstrate the historical validity of their claim. This is written with that object in mind.

The Spoilage, by Thomas and Nishimoto, is a landmark in the orthodox interpretation of Japanese resistance: it is a detailed study of resistance at Tule Lake internment camp, it contains all the orthodox explanations for resistance, and it sets the tone for other studies on the internment camps. Its importance requires a re-examination of the argument employed in that work. Resistance, as characterized by Thomas and Nishimoto, was sporadic and not purposeful, and it was primarily intra-internee rather than anti-administration. The authors cite four basic causes for resistance: (1) the inexperience of the administrators and the initial discomforts of settling in; (2) geo-generational differences and rivalries; (3) conflicts between the old Tuleans and incoming "segregees";[10] and (4) pressure groups of radicals and pro-Axis troublemakers.

For Thomas and Nishimoto, the proof of that interpretation is encapsulated in the vote of January 11, 1944 in which a majority of Tule Lake internees rejected status quo.[11] In that vote there is a statistically significant correlation between blocks which favored status quo and the percentage of segregees. That is, blocks which voted for status quo or the continuation of radical rule had high percentages of segregees in them. That correlation appears to support the authors' contention that protesters and segregees were essentially one and the same. Further, the rejection of status quo came after the radical leaders had been locked away in the stockade. From that, the authors conclude that when given a chance, the people turned to moderate leaders and a conciliatory solution in their desire to return to "normalcy."[12]

The events leading up to that vote in January 1944 and the vote itself, therefore, are crucial to the Thomas and Nishimoto interpretation of resistance and merit a re-examination of those events beginning with the military occupation of Tule Lake on November 4, 1943 and ending with the lifting of martial law on January 15, 1944.[13] Some highlights of that period include the incarceration of the Negotiating Committee, a vote of confidence in those imprisoned leaders despite the administration's efforts to elect new representatives, a hunger strike among the prisoners in the stockade, and the so-called return to normalcy following the vote against status quo.

Ever since the creation of Tule Lake internment camp towards June 1942, the Japanese protested various conditions considered to be unjust. There was a mess hall strike in July, a campaign for higher wages in August, and two labor strikes in August and September. The immediate basis for those protests was the people's concern that they were being doubly exploited by being placed in detention by the government and asked to work to produce their own food for sixteen dollars per month. But the underlying and more fundamental cause of the people's protests was the absurd injustice of their detention.

That was crystallized by the farm labor strike in October 1943 following the accidental death of an internee, Kashima, when a farm truck on which he was riding overturned. To most of the internees, Kashima's death was a senseless loss because he would not have died had there been no internment camp. That mood was reflected in the composition of *Daihyo Sha Kai,* the representative body of the people, in elections which were held the day following Kashima's death. The majority of the sixty-four representatives, one chosen from each block, were individuals who had the reputation of being aggressive opponents of the White administration. Largely because of that and in disregard of their representative nature, the *Daihyo Sha Kai* and the Negotiating Committee were never granted legitimacy by the administrators and instead were seen as antagonists and troublemakers.

When Dillon Myer, the National Director of the WRA, visited Tule Lake the following month, the *Daihyo Sha Kai* resolved to present their complaints directly before him since negotiating with Best, the Tule Lake director, had been shown to be futile. The local bureaucrats denied that request to speak with Myer, and the *Daihyo Sha Kai* decided to force the issue. In a massive show of support, thousands of internees surrounded the administrative building in which Myer was visiting with Best. George Kuratomi, the spokesman of the protesters, outlined to Myer the people's grievances which included Best's dishonest dealings, White racism among certain administrators, inadequate food, overcrowding, and the lack of basic cleaning equipment. But beyond those specific complaints, Kuratomi asked that "we be treated humanely from this Government, this Government of the United States."[14] Myer's response was to align himself firmly with Best and his policies and not give any encouragement to a consideration of the people's demands.

Having failed to receive an acceptable response to their grievances from the WRA, who in the minds of the people were representatives of the United States government, the protesters had no other option but to turn to the Japanese government through the Spanish Consul for redress and support. At this point, there developed a major tactical fracture within the populace. The more conservative protesters who hoped for a post-war future in America viewed the appeal to Japan as incompatible with that desire because White Americans would perceive that to be "un-American." These continued their protest but only through what they considered to be "legitimate" channels — the WRA, the Army, and the Congress. Others who saw no future for themselves and their children in a post-war America viewed the appeal to the Japanese government as their final option. Their first meeting with the Spanish Consul took place on November 3, two days after the confrontation with Myer, and despite his inability to improve the conditions of camp life, the protesters had at least found a receptive ear.

Meanwhile, there was much concern among the White administrators for their personal safety, having witnessed Japanese activism in the mass demonstration of November 1. They demanded military protection in the form of tanks and machine guns, and insisted that a man-proof fence be erected between the administration and internee areas. When Myer and Best failed to give them that reassurance, they went directly to Lt. Col. Verne Austin on November 2 and received Austin's promise that Army troops would guarantee their safety. Best, miffed that his staff went over his head, dismissed two of his most outspoken critics, and within a week twenty staff members resigned.

Best, Myer, and the WRA were confronted with not only internal criticism from their staff for their handling of the mass demonstration of November 1, but also were charged with pampering the Japanese and administrative inefficiency by White residents of the Tule Lake basin and the press, and they faced possible censure from state and national legislative investigating committees. Thus, the November 1 demonstration took on national significance, and the pressure on the WRA to stamp out the resistance seemed to come from factors other than the Japanese protesters themselves. On November 4, following a minor scuffle between a handful of Japanese and White administrators, Best called in the military, a decision which appears to have been precipitated not by the scuffle but by the other pressures mentioned above.[15]

The turning over of the camp to the military, therefore, was a hardening of position *vis-à-vis* resistance and a crackdown against protesters. But Army rule did not end resistance because it failed to rectify the causes of that resistance. Like the WRA, the Army viewed the camp in terms of pressure groups and enemy provocateurs,[16] but unlike the WRA, they were efficient in their repression of Japanese resistance. Individuals were arbitrarily arrested and detained, and there was no recourse or discussion of grievances. Still, throughout the period of military rule, the *Daihyo Sha Kai* urged restraint and open dialogue, but as conditions became progressively more oppressive, their strategy of appealing to the Japanese government was shown to be ineffective and that tactic came increasingly under fire from both extremes of the protest spectrum. On November 12, Austin announced that he no longer recognized the *Daihyo Sha Kai* as the legitimate voice of the people and the following day, he ordered the arrest and detention of members of that representative body.

A tactic employed to stamp out resistance by both the Army and the WRA was to drive a wedge between the majority whom they perceived to be basically co-operative and the minority who were the troublemakers. In a speech on November 13, the day on which the arrest and detention of members of the *Daihyo Sha Kai* began, a WRA official expressed that conspiratorial view: "It is our belief that the majority of the people in this colony do want to live in peace and harmony, that many of you are willing to work and carry on necessary services, but that a few, in order to gain power for themselves, have attempted to gain such power through force."[17]

And in accordance with that strategy of isolating the troublesome minority, the Army, on November 16, reiterated that they did not recognize the *Daihyo Sha Kai* as the legitimate representatives of the people and announced that instead, the block managers would fulfill that function. The block representatives, of whom the *Daihyo Sha Kai* consisted, were elected in free elections sponsored by the people themselves, in contrast with the block managers who had been appointed by the WRA. The Army's reason for recognizing the block managers as their contact with the people was because they are representatives of the WRA. . . ."[18]

That the Army and WRA's conspiratorial view of the camp was grossly inaccurate and that they stubbornly refused to acknowledge the pervasiveness of resistance are clearly illustrated in their meeting with the representatives of the internees on November 18.[19] Austin expressed his suspicion of Japanese motives in the opening statement, that "All discussions held here . . . will be in English throughout the meeting." The block managers, aware of their impossible position, tried to make certain that the administrators understood the mood of the people regarding the announcement of November 16 that they, and not the block representatives, were to be the link with the internees. "We represent the WRA," protested Mayeda, "and we do not represent the people in the colony." Yamatani, a member of the Temporary Communications Committee,[20] added that, "we are still supporting 100% our negotiating committee."[21]

The meeting continued with the block managers pressing the Army on their exact duties since they were henceforth to be the people's representatives. The administrators replied that they were to maintain order[22] and enforce the 6 A.M. to 7 P.M. curfew. Furukawa, a block manager, pointed out that in the past, it was the duty of the wardens and not the block managers to maintain order, and he observed that previously, when the block managers had tried to move constructively to improve the mess halls, the WRA had stifled that initiative. The block managers were trying to get through to the administrators that they were not truly representative of the people and that they did not want to be caught in the middle, being seen as *inu* ("dogs" or "collaborators") by the people for enforcing the administration's unpopular regulations and being powerless to change administrative abuses and excesses.

When the Army tried to press the block managers to commit themselves to maintaining order without giving the assurance that they would have a voice in policy-making, the block managers sought to postpone that commitment by suggesting that they wait until after the expected visit of the Spanish Consul. That led an annoyed Lt. Col. Meek to respond, "We don't need him for negotiating . . ." and, "As far as we are concerned it doesn't make any difference whether he comes or not." Austin reiterated that point and concluded by saying, "Due to conditions that exist in this camp today, the Army is not interested in dealing with the committee with whom we are dealing. We do not believe or feel that it is a representative committee."

The administrators were not interested in dialogue and in understanding the true mood of the people because they had already formed an opinion of that mood. And they were not interested in suggestions about the operation of the camp from internees who held contrary opinions. They were seeking Japanese who reflected their viewpoint and fit into their *a priori* conceptions. Because any internee who was openly critical of the existing order was considered to be subversive by the Army, many were afraid to demonstrate their true inner feelings. That repressive atmosphere created by an arbitrary administration was pointed out by Shirai when he responded,

"Everybody [is] afraid to become a representative on a committee. Afraid that you will pick us up." The pressure to conform was not the monopoly of so-called internee pressure groups, but was a consciously directed policy of the administrators.

Methodical repression of the populace by the Army began the day after that meeting of November 18. Austin, in Proclamation Number 3, required that all internees, twelve years and older, receive identification badges which they had to carry with them at all times.[23] And on November 22, a comprehensive plan was formulated for a massive search of the Japanese area to be carried out on November 26. Among the stated purposes for that search were: (a) the taking into custody of trouble-making Japanese;[24] and (b) the confiscating of contraband such as knives, clubs, guns, explosives, and signalling devices. The search was to be carried out by three groups of about 150 men, each soldier carrying full field equipment and a gas mask, and every officer having side arms, clubs, and gas grenades.

The block managers were informed of this search only on the designated day, when the raid was launched with the precision of a well-planned military maneuver. The soldiers netted 25 tons of rice and other grains, 22 barrels of *saké* mash, 400 boxes of canned goods, 20 crates of dried fruit, 20 cartons of cereal, 2 *saké* stills, a Japanese language printing press, 500 knives, 400 clubs, 2 public address systems, and 500 radio receivers.[25]

Meanwhile on November 24, Austin and Best concurred on the erecting of a stockade which would include four barracks for the incarceration of "troublemakers." Various lists of such persons were drawn up and these were methodically hunted down and placed in detention in the stockade not having been charged or given a hearing. On December 4, Austin announced to the people, "You are notified that the members of the negotiating committee now in military custody are not and will not at any time negotiate with the Army, the WRA, or anyone else and they will not return to the colony." He therefore advised that the people hold elections for a new representative committee.[26]

The same day, the block representatives met to discuss Austin's suggestion and decided that they would place the matter before the people. There were three questions on the ballot the following day, December 5. These were: (1) should the *Daihyo Sha Kai* be dissolved and new representatives be elected to negotiate with the Army?; (2) should status quo be maintained? (i.e. should we support our present block representatives and the Negotiating Committee?); and (3) should there be a general strike in support of those who were imprisoned in the stockade? The results of that day's voting were as follows: three blocks favored a general strike, three blocks voted for new elections, five blocks remained undecided, and fifty-three blocks favored status quo.[27] Despite the administrators' coercive tactics, the referendum of December 5 was evidence of an overwhelming vote of confidence in the *Daihyo Sha Kai* and the Negotiating Committee.

But the pressures against maintaining status quo continued to build up the longer the Army remained intransigent in releasing members of the Negotiating Committee from the stockade and insisted on dealing only with a new committee of internees. That hopeless deadlock was pointed out by the Spanish Consul on December 13 at a meeting with the people, when he urged that the internees elect a new negotiating committee because the present Committee was powerless to effect change while in the stockade.[28] Despite that recommendation, few of the Japanese ventured to express support publicly, fearing to be viewed as pro-administration and against the imprisoned but still *de facto* leaders of the people. Yet, by isolating the members of the Negotiating Committee from the camp, the Army made it difficult for the leaders to communicate with the people.

Between the end of December 1943 and the beginning of January 1944, a series of events occurred which brought the situation to a head. According to one account, on the morning of December 30, Lt. Schaner, the Police and Prisoner Officer, arbitrarily took Yoshiyama and Tsuda, two prisoners, from the general stockade and confined them to a small cell within the stockade enclosure.[29] Schaner himself had selected these two previously to be the spokesmen for the prisoners, and his high-handed confinement of them reinforced the arbitrary manner in which the White administrators disregarded the internees' human rights.[30] In protest of Schaner's harassment of prisoners, the stockaders refused to assemble for the roll call at 1300.

One of the prisoners, Mori, spoke with Schaner about the situation and received the latter's promise that Yoshiyama and Tsuda would be released if the prisoners cleaned up the stockade area and assembled for the evening roll call. The Japanese fulfilled those conditions but by the next morning, Yoshiyama and Tsuda still had not been released. To protest that breach of promise the prisoners refused to assemble for roll call that day, December 31, but only after armed troops were brought into the stockade later in the day did the Japanese yield and file out of their barracks.

At the roll call, Schaner again arbitrarily pointed to a prisoner, Uchida, and ordered him to be confined to the small stockade along with Yoshiyama and Tsuda. Then he challenged the Japanese, "Now if there are any more of you who would like to go with him, just step up towards the gate." After a moment's pause, one of them, Koji Todoroki, stepped forward and according to an Army eyewitness, "a murmur passed through the prisoners, followed by the entire group breaking ranks and moving in the direction of the gate."[31]

The men were forced to remain in line and stand in the snow for about three hours during which time Schaner conferred with Austin. Schaner returned to announce to the prisoners, "I was just waiting for that. You men will be put on bread and water for twenty-four hours. You men will have to learn that we mean business and will not tolerate such a demonstration."[32] Trucks then entered the stockade and removed all stores of foodstuffs. One of the Japanese brought in from the outside to help load the trucks showed a reluctance to carry out that task, and he received "a few *tender* cuffs from Lt. Smith and S/Sgt. Anderson which made him change his mind." Meanwhile, Schaner ordered a search of the prisoners' quarters, which was conducted, according to one military observer, "in a most unnecessary destructive method."[33] Many personal items were stolen from the Japanese including radios, pens, watches, cigarettes, and cash.

Following that display of flagrant abuse and disregard of their rights, the prisoners vowed to go on a hunger strike until the release of all prisoners in the stockade. One of the prisoners, Tsuda, explained why that decision was made. "The reason the men . . . are on this hunger strike is because they know not the reason they are in the stockade. They feel they have been unjustly confined and the reason given to them is that they are the potential troublemakers and strong arm men of the colony, which they feel is not true. This is the manner in which they are trying to prove their sincerity and show that they should be vindicated."[34] The prisoners were protesting the arbitrary nature of their arrest and confinement, and they were trying to point out to the administrators once again their error in seeing the camp in terms of pressure groups and enemy provocateurs.

To the internees, the entire situation was absurd and senseless. In the first place, their removal and internment was an absurd though hardly unexpected happening. The White camp administrators, while accusing the Japanese of using pressure groups, employed high-handed and terror tactics in dealing with internee protest against what they considered to be violations of their fundamental human rights. Further, the administrators stubbornly refused to examine the protesters' demands objectively, rejected out of hand the legitimacy of the people's chosen representatives, and equated any criticism of their administration with pro-Axis sentiments and saw them as subversive and destructive of the American war effort.

At the same time, those same administrators lectured to the internees about the virtues of American democracy while incarcerating those who had been elected democratically by the people and who were exercising those rights of democracy. To the Japanese, there was no rational basis for the existence of the stockade or the presence of tanks and soldiers in the camp. The entire situation could have been simply resolved had the administrators accepted the legitimacy of the *Daihyo Sha Kai,* shown sincerity in discussing camp problems, and treated the internees as people with basic human rights.[35]

The prisoners' hunger strike lasted from January 1 to January 6, 1944 without producing any tangible concessions from the administration. The administrators kept the camp population ignorant of the protest until the third day of the strike when a group of concerned internees asked Austin about "rumors" of a hunger strike among the stockade prisoners and Austin confirmed its veracity. Despite an anonymously authored call among the internees for a demonstration of solidarity with the hunger strikers, there is no evidence of any such visible show of support.[36] Instead, the available sources show that there was a growing sentiment among the populace against status quo in an attempt to break the current deadlock.

There are several interesting features in the argument employed against status quo. Keeping in mind that the official (WRA and Army) and orthodox explanation is that the movement against status quo indicated that the majority of the internees rejected the legitimacy of the *Daihyo Sha Kai* and Negotiating Committee and simply wished for a return to "normalcy," we will examine some of those features. The basic premise of the argument against status quo was that the people were being severely oppressed, both in the stockade and in the camp, since martial rule. The *Daihyo Sha Kai,* the argument continued, had failed to alleviate that oppression, both because they were not recognized by the administrators and because they were being held prisoners in the stockade. Therefore, the argument concluded, a new committee must be elected, one leading to improved camp conditions and the release of those in the stockade.

The argument here was a practical one: It was not a rejection of the *Daihyo Sha Kai* as the legitimate representatives of the people but was a recognition of the impasse and that this solution was the only option permitted by the administrators. Further, their appeal was not to American patriotism but to Japanese ethnicity. The members of the *Daihyo Sha Kai,* the argument went, were not displaying the "true Japanese spirit" because "true" Japanese would resign having failed. And the appeal concluded, "we have no other desire than to exist as a true Japanese and to return to Japan unashamed."[37]

On January 10, Austin sent out a memorandum to the block managers with instructions on the upcoming referendum which was to decide on the question of status quo. That there would arise confusion among many of the internees on the issue being voted upon was assured by Austin's instructions to the block managers. These instructions failed to be accompanied by a sample ballot, and one of them stated: "Whenever any questions should arise from the floor the chair should state that he is not in a position to answer them. The only purpose of the meeting is to have the block residents vote on the question listed on the ballots."[38] The following day, January 11, Austin held a meeting with all the block managers to discuss the voting which was to take place that night. At the meeting, he reinforced the notion that should the people vote against status quo, military oppression would end. "A great deal depends upon the manner in which these meetings are held," Austin admonished, "as to whether this colony comes back to normal, in which I believe you are all interested."[39]

That night, voting was held in the camp with the ballots simply labelled, "Against Status Quo" and "For Status Quo." The results of the voting as reported by the Army was, 4,593 against status quo, 4,120 for, and 228 undecided.[40] One internee report disputed that count and accused the administrators of rigging the election results because no internees were present at the tabulation of the votes. That report went on to claim that a true count was, thirty-one blocks for status quo, twenty-nine blocks against, four blocks undetermined, and one block abstained.[41] Also, one of the internees later testified that "the ballots were none too good and some people didn't understand the meaning of status quo."[42] But apart from the question of the validity of the results, the vote revealed the reluctance of the people to cast a vote which could be interpreted as being a repudiation of the *Daihyo Sha Kai* despite the argument that such a vote would be followed by the release of the men in the stockade and a lessening of military oppression.

In a meeting held on January 14 between those who had favored the abolishing of status quo and *Daihyo Sha Kai* members who were in the stockade, their unity of purpose was reaffirmed although they had chosen two different approaches to that one basic goal.[43] Both groups lamented the fact that the issue had split the internees. "I surely hate to see the Japanese divided," commented Inouye, "and hate to see them fighting with each other." Shimada explained why that division was brought about and why they had voted against status quo. "Let me repeat this," he asserted, "the Army would not give a chance to talk about [the] release of you people, unless normal condition was first returned." Inouye, a spokesman for the stockade prisoners, reconfirmed the unity of purpose of both groups and offered: "We realize all the things you people are going through and have told the men in the stockade that you people were working so hard for the common goal. We are just as worried as you people are."

On January 15, 1944, just four days after the status quo referendum, the Army formally turned over the administration of Tule Lake internment camp to the WRA, ostensibly after having fulfilled their mission of stamping out resistance. They had accomplished that by isolating the troublemakers from the majority of the people and were vindicated in the recent referendum which they interpreted as being a repudiation of the *Daihyo Sha Kai* and a vote for the return to "normalcy." Austin expressed his persistent belief in the orthodox view of resistance on the eve of his departure: "The block representatives were all appointees of the pressure group and while some of them were capable and responsible members of the Colony the rest were actively engaged in fomenting unrest, discord and recommending violence to those desiring a return of normalcy within the Colony."[44]

While the period of military rule is merely a limited window into Japanese resistance at Tule Lake, it is a time segment crucial to the orthodox interpretation of resistance. That interpretation maintains that it was during that repressive period that the internee majority were permitted to express themselves freely because of the incarceration of the radicals, and that expression was a rejection of status quo and the election of moderate leaders.

In contrast, it can be seen that there had been a history of resistance and there was no such dramatic break, because both groups, for and against status quo, were committed to a program of reform and the continuing fight for a recognition of their humanity. Their disagreement was in the method of resistance. One group believed that the release of prisoners in the stockade was the first step toward a peaceful relationship between internees and administrators, while the other group held that the latter would be followed by the former. Further, the vote against status quo was not necessarily a vote against the *Daihyo Sha Kai*. In fact, the leaders in that vote saw it as a practical solution to the impasse created by the administration's intransigence. And in the final analysis, both those who favored status quo and those opposed to it were united in the underlying and pervasive struggle for human rights.

Notes

1. See e.g., Morton Grodzins, *Americans Betrayed* (Chicago, 1949); Jacobus ten-Broek, Edward N. Barnhart, and Floyd W. Matson, *Prejudice, War, and the Constitution* (Berkeley, 1954); and Roger Daniels, *Concentration Camps, USA* (New York, 1971).

2. See e.g., Dorothy Swaine Thomas and Richard S. Nishimoto, *The Spoilage* (Berkeley, 1946).

3. See e.g., Leonard J. Arrington, *The Price of Prejudice* (Logan, Utah, 1962); Bill Hosokawa, *Nisei: The Quiet Americans* (New York, 1969); and Harry H. L. Kitano, *Japanese Americans: The Evolution of a Subculture* (Englewood Cliffs, New Jersey, 1969).

4. Edward H. Spicer, Asael T. Hansen, Katherine Luomala, and Marvin K. Opler, *Impounded People* (Tucson, 1969), pp. 15–16, 23, 63–64; and Alexander H. Leighton, *The Governing of Men* (Princeton, 1945), pp. 90–92.

5. Carey McWilliams, *Prejudice* (Boston, 1944), pp. 173, 176; Dillon S. Myer, *Uprooted Americans* (Tucson, 1971), pp. 59–65; and Shotaro Frank Miyamoto, "A Study of the Career of Intergroup Tensions: The Collective Adjustments of Evacuees to Crises at the Tule Lake Relocation Center," Ph.D. diss., University of Chicago, 1950.

6. McWilliams, *Prejudice,* 177–78; Paul Bailey, *City in the Sun* (Los Angeles, 1971); and Thomas and Nishimoto, *The Spoilage.*

7. McWilliams, *Prejudice,* pp. 179–80; and Thomas and Nishimoto, *The Spoilage.*

8. Douglas W. Nelson, "Heart Mountain: The History of an American Concentration Camp," M.A. thesis, University of Wyoming, 1970; Gary Y. Okihiro, "Japanese Resistance in America's Concentration Camps: A Re-evaluation," *Amerasia Journal,* 2

(Fall 1973), 20–34; and Arthur A. Hansen and David A. Hacker, "The Manzanar Riot: An Ethnic Perspective," *Amerasia Journal,* 2 (Fall 1974), 112–57.

9. As done for the Chinese in Alexander Saxton's *The Indispensable Enemy* (Berkeley, 1971).

10. Tule Lake became a "segregation center" after September 1943 following the so-called loyalty registration which segregated the internees into "loyals" and "disloyals." Those who were designated as "disloyals" were termed "segregees" and transferred to Tule Lake internment camp.

11. "Status quo" was the continuation of the *Daihyo Sha Kai* and Negotiating Committee as the legitimate representatives of the people. The *Daihyo Sha Kai* had been formed in October 1943 by a free and democratic election of all the internees of Tule Lake camp. Its composition, in the words of Thomas and Nishimoto, consisted of "belligerent, vociferous individuals who had gained the reputation of being aggressive opponents of the administration. . . ." The Negotiating Committee was composed of fourteen members of the *Daihyo Sha Kai* who were nominated to serve as the larger body's mouthpiece in negotiations with the administration. Thomas and Nishimoto, *The Spoilage,* p. 117.

12. Thomas and Nishimoto, *The Spoilage,* pp. 184–86.

13. A separate paper to be published in a forthcoming edited volume covers the period before martial law.

14. "Transcript of the Meeting," November 1, 1943, in Japanese American Research Project, Collection 2010, Research Library, University of California, Los Angeles [henceforth referred to as JARP Collection], Austin Papers, Box 43 [henceforth referred to as AP], Folder 4, Document 3.

15. Oral history interview with Dillon S. Myer, May 20, 1968, in JARP Collection, AP, Box 397, No. 300.

16. The orthodox interpretation of resistance falls into this same error. Protest, by the WRA and Army, was seen as being anti-administration and disruptive. In its most extreme form, the WRA and Army viewed themselves as representatives of the American government. Resistance, therefore, was anti-American and even disruptive of the entire war effort. To the internees, protest was constructive and designed simply to gain a recognition of their fundamental human rights and for a more satisfactory life in the camps. As evidence of this contrast, see Leighton, *Governing of Men,* pp. 81–89; and Spicer et al., *Impounded,* p. 133, in which at Poston, members of the WRA staff equated the internees with the Japanese enemy.

17. Speech by Mr. Cozzens, November 13, 1943, in JARP Collection, AP, Folder 5, Document 23.

18. Notes by Lt. Forbes at a meeting held November 16, 1943, in JARP Collection, AP, Folder 5, Document 27.

19. The proceedings of this meeting were taken from Evacuee Meeting, November 18, 1943, in JARP Collection, AP, Folder 6, Document 1.

20. The Temporary Communications Committee had been appointed by the *Daihyo Sha Kai* to serve as their representatives throughout the period of their detention by the Army.

21. As noted before, the Negotiating Committee consisted of fourteen members nominated from among the *Daihyo Sha Kai* to serve as the mouthpiece of that representative body.

22. Proclamation Number 2, November 13, 1943, spelled out some of the regulations which were to be enforced. These included the prohibiting of outdoor meet-

ings without prior military approval, and no incoming or outgoing telephone or telegraph messages without administrative consent. JARP Collection, AP, Folder 5, Document 18.

23. Proclamation Number 3, November 19, 1943, in JARP Collection, AP, Folder 6, Document 4.

24. Various members of the Negotiating Committee had successfully eluded arrest by the Army by going into hiding. These included Kuratomi, Kai, and Sugimoto.

25. JARP Collection, AP, Folder 6, Documents 7, 11, 15, 17.

26. Notice to All Residents of Tule Lake Center, December 12, 1943, in JARP Collection, AP, Folder 7, Document 6.

27. JARP Collection, AP, Folder 7, Document 7. Cf. "Minutes of the Meeting of the Dai-Hyo Sha Kai of the Tule Lake Center," December 5, 1943, in the Bancroft Library collection of material relating to the evacuation and internment, University of California, Berkeley, Folder R 2.25, which records the final vote to be: three blocks for a general strike, four blocks for new elections, two blocks were undecided, and fifty-six blocks for status quo.

28. JARP Collection, AP, Folder 7, Document 17. Another indication that the internees were trying all avenues open to them was their petition to the U.S. Secretary of War, Henry L. Stimson, dated December 7, 1943. The petition summarized the events which led to the military occupation of Tule Lake and asked for administrative co-operation and dialogue. JARP Collection, AP, Folder 7, Document 32.

29. Another account states that these men were confined to the small stockade because they had laughed out loud during the calling of the roll. Yoshiyama and Tsuda, however, were not laughing at the White soldiers but at two men who were trying to load cartons of tobacco. JARP Collection, AP, Folder 8, Document 26.

30. See e.g., JARP Collection, AP, Folder 8, Document 24.

31. "Stockade Prisoners Rebellion," an investigation by S/Sgt. Sam Yeramian, December 31, 1943, in JARP Collection, AP, Folder 7, Document 30.

32. "Stockade Prisoners Rebellion."

33. "Stockade Prisoners Rebellion."

34. Interview with Hiroyoshi Tsuda, January 5, 1944, in JARP Collection, AP, Folder 8, Document 8.

35. Interview with Hiroyoshi Tsuda; and "Meeting of the Spanish Consul," November 3, 1943, in JARP Collection, AP, Folder 4, Document 4.

36. "Voice of the People," in JARP Collection, AP, Folder 8, Document 10.

37. JARP Collection, AP, Folder 8, Documents 15, 16, 17, 19, 20.

38. Memorandum, Austin to Block Managers, January 10, 1944, in JARP Collection, AP, Folder 8, Document 18. The block managers were to read a statement from a pamphlet prepared by the administration to the assembled people immediately before the voting began. Unfortunately, there is no record of what that statement said. "Minutes of a General Meeting of all Block Managers," January 11, 1944, in JARP Collection, AP, Folder 8, Document 21.

39. "Minutes of a General Meeting of all Block Managers," January 11, 1944.

40. JARP Collection, AP, Folder 8, Document 22. Despite the statistically significant correlation between blocks voting for status quo and the percentage of segregees in those blocks, the link is not necessarily a causal one.

41. "Report of Present Condition," by the Nippon Patriotic Society, in JARP Collection, AP, Folder 8, Document 29. This protest of the official count is important when one considers the 228 listed by the Army as "undecided." If, for instance, that

228 and the 247 disenfranchised stockade prisoners voted for status quo, those favoring status quo would have a majority of 4,595 to 4,593.

42. "Report of the Informal Interview of the Divisional Responsible Men and the Detained Stockade Internees," January 14, 1944, in JARP Collection, AP, Folder 8, Document 26. On the morning of the vote, soldiers rounded up some members of the *Daihyo Sha Kai* and status quo sympathizers. That may have influenced a number of the Japanese to vote in conformance with the Army's wishes. Thomas and Nishimoto, *The Spoilage,* pp. 181–82.

43. The proceedings of this meeting were taken from "Report of the Informal Interview," January 14, 1944.

44. Letter from Austin to de Amat, January 14, 1944, in JARP Collection, AP, Folder 8, Document 27.

5. What was the impact of
internment on Japanese American
families and communities?

Valerie J. Matsumoto

Amache

This selection by Valerie Matsumoto demonstrates how oral history sources can enrich internment historiography. Only in the past two decades have many former internees been willing to share their histories with the public. Many broke their silence because of the campaign for redress, highlighted by the 1981 Commission on Wartime Relocation and Internment of Civilians hearings and the 1988 Civil Liberties Act, which awarded surviving internees $20,000 and a national apology. The redress movement encouraged Japanese Americans to speak about the war before the government, to write memoirs, and to recount their oral histories to researchers.

Matsumoto was a history graduate student at Stanford in 1982 when she heard that an agricultural community in California's San Joaquin Valley was looking for a scholar to conduct a history project for them. She learned that this community, the Cortez colony, was one of three planned Christian colonies established by businessman Abiko Kyutaro. During the war, the colonists had hired a white manager to oversee their farms and thus were able to preserve their landholdings while interned at the Amache camp. They also maintained a large network of religious, civic, and social organizations. Ignoring WRA advice to disperse throughout the country, this community remained intact for three generations when it began looking for a historian. Excited at the prospect of working with this unique community, Matsumoto eagerly asked to be considered for the position.

Her heart sank when she heard that Cortez, unable to agree on whether to produce a film, book, exhibit, or slide show, had decided to cancel the project. "About ten minutes into the beginning of deep despair," Matsumoto realized that "the Cortez residents had not said they did not want a history project, only that they were not going to carry it out themselves."[1] She got in touch with the community and found two families willing to serve as her "home bases" as she worked around the seasonal farm schedule conducting interviews for her dissertation. Nobuzo and Miye Baba showed Matsumoto "the Growers Association building, the JACL Hall, and the two churches, and then commenced calling their neighbors to see who would agree to be interviewed." While the Babas introduced Matsumoto to many Buddhists in town, George and Helen Yuge helped her meet the Christians in the community. To facilitate contacts and set up interviews, the two families took Matsumoto to numerous events, ranging from a Boy Scouts' fund-raising pancake breakfast to a local JACL installation banquet.

Although Matsumoto also used organizational records, newspapers, and wartime memorabilia in her research, her eighty three interviews clearly yielded the richest material for the dissertation that became *Farming the Home Place* (1993). She used these oral histories to explore gender role development, generational change and continuity, ethnic support networks, and the functions of community before, during, and after the war. She also found that there was no single, "representative" response to internment. Earlier studies portraying internees as either victims or protesters de-emphasized their diverse backgrounds and experiences. Matsumoto discovered that even a seemingly homogeneous community like Cortez was divided by generational and gender issues during the war. Internment accelerated some Nisei's quest for greater independence and weakened patriarchal authority. As Issei men lost their role as family breadwinner and were barred from political positions, more Nisei refused to abide by arranged marriages. Nisei men and women also became more assertive as they left camp for the armed forces, jobs, or college.

Matsumoto's oral histories also show that the Nisei men and women from Cortez had a wide range of attitudes and responses that defy simple categorization. Earlier accounts portrayed internees as either heroic soldiers, assimilated Americans, browbeaten victims, or militant protesters. But Matsumoto found that one picture cannot capture the diverse reactions to internment. Instead, in this selection on the Amache camp, she provides a composite portrait of individuals using networks of friends and relatives to cope with internment in a variety of ways.

Matsumoto acknowledges that her relationships with her interviewees may have affected their representations of the past. "As a researcher," she explains in her introduction to *Farming the Home Place,* "I was both an insider and an outsider."

> While I did not grow up in Cortez or in a Japanese American community, my background as a Sansei woman whose parents had raised tomatoes in southern California gave me some familiarity with Japanese American culture and the rhythms of rural life. At the beginning of each interview, I was asked where my family came from and in which camp they had been interned. I replied that my grandparents came from Fukuoka-ken in southern Japan, that they and their children had farmed in northern and southern California, and that they had spent the war years in the Poston Camp in Arizona and the Topaz Camp in Utah. These facts enabled the Cortez people to locate me within the Japanese American cosmos and to confirm the presence of common bonds of understanding between us.

Never pretending to be an "objective" researcher, Matsumoto candidly admits that her perspective on Cortez was influenced by a sense that "its history and hospitality were intertwined." In an appendix to the book titled "Notes on Research," she describes trying to alleviate any anxiety her interviewees might have experienced by sending her questions (also included in the book's appendix) ahead of time and agreeing to omit any topics they disliked. Aware that she was the same age as many of her interviewees' children, she always "remained conscious of the bonds of responsibility and affection."

According to Matsumoto, "One must examine one's priorities as a scholar, and weigh the implications of one's work for the women and men whose history has formed its bedrock." In *Farming the Home Place,* an article on Nisei women during the war,[2] and an article on Nisei women writers of the 1930s,[3] Matsumoto has helped restore the voices and experiences of Japanese American women to the pages of history. She is a professor in the history department at the University of California at Los Angeles and in 1992 led an interdisciplinary seminar for UCLA faculty on integrating internment into their curricula. A mainstay of UCLA's Asian American Studies Program, she also has cultivated some of the most promising new scholars in the field.

Questions for a Closer Reading

1. Matsumoto notes that "Amache was considered to be one of the more peaceful" camps. How does she account for this? What might explain the differences between Amache and Tule Lake?

2. Using her oral histories, Matsumoto profiles a number of reactions to internment and resettlement. Compare the ways people describe life in the camp, in military service, at college, and at work outside the camp. Why do you think people had such different views and experiences?

3. What role did the internees' networks of relatives and friends play in their adjusting to internment and resettlement?

4. Matsumoto repeatedly quotes her oral histories, but she also supplements these interviews with other sources. At one point, she contrasts memories shared during interviews with wartime letters. Why might memories in oral history sources not always be reliable? How can a scholar balance the use of such sources with other kinds of evidence?

5. Matsumoto declares, "It is impossible to summarize neatly the wartime experiences and feelings of even one family or community, much less the entire Japanese American population." How does her research challenge earlier generalizations of the consequences of internment?

Notes

1. Valerie Matsumoto, "Notes on Research," *Farming the Home Place: A Japanese American Community in California, 1919–1982* (Ithaca, N.Y.: Cornell University Press, 1993), p. 220.

2. "Desperately Seeking 'Deirdre': Gender Roles, Multicultural Relations, and Nisei Women Writers of the 1930s," *Frontiers* 12, No. 1 (1991): 19–32.

3. "Japanese American Women during World War II," *Frontiers* 8, No. 1 (1984): 6–14.

Amache

At the end of August 1942, the Merced Assembly Center evacuees reached Amache, Colorado. Their last stop on the train from California was the town of Granada, Colorado, population 342, established as an Indian trading post in 1844. The evacuees were taken by truck from the railroad station to the nearby Granada Relocation Center, named Amache after the daughter of a Cheyenne Indian chief whose tribe had lived along the Arkansas River.[1]

The Amache Camp in southeastern Colorado, roughly one mile southwest of the Arkansas Valley, was one of ten "permanent" relocation centers constructed in desolate regions under the auspices of the War Relocation Authority (WRA) to house Japanese Americans. The Merced evacuees arrived five months after the first Japanese Americans had been moved from the temporary assembly centers to WRA camps. Amache was the smallest of the camps, with a capacity of 8,000 residents. Most of the camps held 10,000 and the largest, the Poston Camp in Arizona, contained 20,000 people in three units.[2] By November of 1942, all the relocation centers were filled.

Four months later — a year after President Roosevelt had signed Executive Order 9066 — Dillon S. Myer, head of the War Relocation Authority, issued a statement censuring the "unnatural" and "un-American" environment of the relocation centers. Myer particularly cited the disruption of the Japanese American family by the lack of privacy and by the absence of normal family economy and home routines, which led to a corresponding decline in parental authority. He concluded that the camps were "undesirable institutions and should be removed from the American scene as soon as possible."[3]

Valerie J. Matsumoto, "Amache," *Farming the Home Place: A Japanese American Community in California, 1919–1982* (Ithaca, N.Y.: Cornell University Press, 1993), 119–48.

The relocation camps subjected families and individuals to severe stress. In accordance with many earlier scholars and observers, the congressional Commission on Wartime Relocation and Internment of Civilians reported in 1982: "The human toll the camps were taking was enormous — physical hardship, growing anger toward the United States and deteriorating morale."[4] Previous patterns of life — and the most fundamental relationships — underwent great change. As Audrie Girdner and Anne Loftis have pointed out, "the economic and social basis of the Issei's authority had been abolished by the welfare system under which all residents lived."[5] The cramped barracks, mess-hall dining, and increased peer-group interaction meant that family members spent less and less time together. In addition to the strain on family relationships, evacuees coped with internal rivalries arising between groups from different regions of the West Coast, as well as more general concerns regarding low-paying camp jobs, isolation, and negative public sentiment on the "outside."[6]

Amache was considered to be one of the more peaceful relocation centers, located in an inland area described by Michi Weglyn as "less unnerved by racially slanted media bombardment" and farther from the hostile racial climate of Arizona and California.[7] Even at best, however, as Robert Wilson and Bill Hosokawa have stated, "camp life was abnormal — subject to uncertainty, fear, frustration, anger, emotional pressures, great physical discomfort, resentment, and beset by an abundance of rumors that fed on boredom and bitterness."[8] While pondering an uncertain future, the internees strove to meet the physically and psychologically exhausting demands of daily life in a concentration camp.

How did camp life affect the Japanese Americans? The first half of this chapter explores conditions within the Amache Camp, particularly focusing on the factors that made many evacuees eager to leave and rejoin life on the "outside." Even before the last evacuees had moved into the relocation centers, Myer and the WRA had decided to focus on resettlement out of the camps. Although the WRA's leave-clearance process proved initially cumbersome and slow, the first Japanese Americans began to trek out of the camps to the Midwest and East in 1942. The wartime demand for labor and the changes in WRA policy increased this trickle to a steady stream in 1943. The ranks of the hopeful men and women who left the camps for army duty, education, and work included a number of Cortez Nisei, whose lives beyond barbed wire illustrate the paths taken by the Nisei as well as the establishment of friend and kin networks upon which the relocating evacuees depended for emotional support and assistance.

Ernest Yoshida, a Nisei from the Cortez Colony, recalled the arduous trip to Amache. Despite the suffocating heat on the crowded train, armed guards would not allow the Japanese Americans to open windows. "We got to Bakersfield, and it got hotter and hotter. Then the train started pulling toward Tehachapi Mountain, and it got hotter, and the kids started crying." In the evening, when the Japanese Americans wanted to pull down the Pullman beds for the children to sleep on, the guards ordered them to "leave those things alone." The adults stood in the aisles so that the children could stretch out and sleep in the seats.

In the course of the two-day trip, the evacuees were permitted two twenty-minute rest breaks during which they could get off the train and stretch but were warned not to go beyond four feet from the train. "I think when we got to Arizona, they finally stopped. By that time the kids were sick and the old folks were half-dead. Then, when we got off, here are all the guards standing guard with machine guns, so that we couldn't run away. Crazy, I tell you."

Yoshida continued:

The kids started hollering for water, and we didn't have any water. It was hot and dry. And finally we reached Granada Station . . . two days, no bath and no water. It was four o'clock [in the afternoon], so we thought we had plenty of time to get off the train and go to the camp. "No," they said, "the camp isn't ready until tomorrow morning. . . . You have to stay overnight on the train." And we said, "Where are we going to sleep? You guys won't let us take the bunks down." "Well, that's the orders—we don't know what to do about it."

The following morning, the advance group of Japanese Americans who had arrived at the Amache Camp days earlier came to pick up the new arrivals in trucks. The weary Issei and Nisei set about moving into their new barracks, looking for straw to stuff mattresses, and locating the shower rooms, latrines, and mess halls. "That night we all slept like a log. The next morning we got up, and then the same old routine — nothing to do. Maybe go to a neighbor's, play cards. And those that wanted to . . . went to the scrap pile and picked up wood, and made shelves and desks. . . . That's the way we passed the time away."[9] Ernest Yoshida, like many of the evacuated Nisei, chafed at the confines of the camp and made plans to leave as soon as possible to seek opportunities on the "outside."

The Amache Camp was located within the southern boundary of a mile-square enclosure overlooking the Arkansas River. On the west lay a cemetery, dump pile, and sewer farm, and on the east, a prairie extending into Kansas. Along the northern boundary were a hospital, warehouses, housing for the appointed staff, administration buildings, and a military police compound.[10]

Life at Amache paralleled life in the assembly center with regard to organization, although the camp population was larger and the Colorado weather more extreme — many Californians saw their first snow in Amache. As in the Merced Assembly Center, the "evacuee residential section" was divided into blocks. Each of the twenty-nine blocks had its own mess hall, laundry, latrine, shower room, and recreation hall. The center also housed several churches — Buddhist and Christian — an elementary school, and a high school, for which a special building was constructed a year after the camp opened.

Each block was comprised of twelve barracks, 20 × 120 feet, each divided into six one-room "apartments." A family of seven members or less was assigned to a room and "allowed to make it as homelike as possible."[11] The barracks eventually had brick floors, although some of the first arrivals found only dirt beneath their feet. The government sparsely furnished each apartment with steel army cots, a broom, a pot-bellied stove, and a coal bucket. Making a room "homelike" generally consisted of scavenging the lumber piles for scraps to make furniture, and partitioning spaces with blankets to provide a semblance of privacy.

Like the assembly center, the relocation camp contained a mixture of rural and urban residents. Approximately half of the Amache Camp inhabitants hailed from the Los Angeles area and had been funneled through the Santa Anita Assembly Center. These included urban merchants, doctors, lawyers, scientists, gardeners, and hotel and restaurant operators. The other half, sent from the Merced Assembly Center, were predominantly rural people from the agricultural sections of the central California valleys and the San Francisco Bay Area. Forty percent of the evacuees had been engaged in agriculture; 15 percent did domestic work; 10 percent held professional and managerial positions; 13 percent had done clerical and sales work. Sixteen percent did semiskilled labor, and 6 percent unskilled.[12] At its population peak in 1943, Amache had 7,318 residents.[13]

About 260 Cortez people entered the Amache Camp, and the majority lived in Blocks 9E and 10E. Even among old friends and relatives, living so close together necessitated a certain amount of rearranging, as Sam Kuwahara learned. "I remember helping arrange the people moving into different barracks. I was all wrong. . . . They shifted around quite a bit. We thought relatives would want to stay together—naw, they didn't want to do that [Laughs]."[14]

The residents of the city that rose so quickly and completely from the prairie continued to follow the patterns of life established at the Merced Assembly Center, filling time with work, social and religious activities, classes, athletic and cultural events, and visiting. Amache, too, was run like a model city, through a series of departments headed by Euro-American administrators, with James Lindley, formerly of the Soil Conservation Corps as project director. As in the assembly center, there existed an internal fire department and police department, staffed by Japanese Americans.

In Amache, a community council of elected representatives became an established body. This contrasted with the situation at the Merced Assembly Center, where the vacillations of the Wartime Civil Control Administration (WCCA) — and the short period of duration — had hindered such attempts. In the relocation camp, members of each block who were eighteen years and older voted for a representative to the council, which was charged with "the prescription of ordinances, regulations, and laws governing community life within the center." In addition, a judicial commission of three administrative personnel and five Japanese Americans heard and tried cases regarding the violation of rules.[15] However, scholars have questioned the efficacy of such attempts at "community self-government," contending that elected representatives had little authority to effect change, and that the policy itself — by making only citizens eligible for election — widened the divisions between Issei and Nisei, vying for leadership.[16] As the Commission on Wartime Relocation and Internment of Civilians concluded, "many evacuees regarded the system as a sham, further evidence that they were not trusted, and an example of bad faith by the WRA."[17]

Each block also had a block manager, usually Issei, to oversee administrative matters. The duties of the manager, nominated by the residents but appointed by the project director, included handling requests for housing, heating, and household supplies, and relaying announcements and instructions from the administration. The other block staff person was the personnel director, in charge of the population and occupational records files. It was his job to facilitate labor recruitment, to ensure adequate distribution of food, to keep track of migration in and out of the camp, and to record vital statistics.[18]

Amache had a large educational program, similar to the other relocation camps.[19] In January 1944, the enrollment included 199 nursery school children, 802 kindergartners and elementary school pupils, 433 junior high school students, 549 high school students, and 1,043 enrollees in the adult school. The school staff consisted of three principals, a superintendent, fifty-one WRA teachers, and forty-four Japanese American assistant teachers. Except for the high school, classes were held in remodeled barracks, and adult classes — ranging from sewing to English — met in the high school building or in special rooms of the 8H school block.

Envisioned as a longer-term project than the assembly centers, the Amache Camp had several internal enterprises: a silk-screen printing shop, cooperative stores, and a large agricultural section. Because of the WRA's early decision to encourage relocation outside of the camps and its desire not to compete with the industrial production of private business on the outside, most of the enterprises established within the relocation centers were geared to internal consumption. A notable exception was the Amache Silk Screen Shop, organized in June of 1943 at the request of the United States Navy. It was the only such project in all of the relocation centers. The forty-five evacuees who worked in the shop under the supervision of a WRA administrator contracted with the Navy to print thousands of training-aid posters. They also produced a calendar that prominently featured an Amache guard tower, as well as covers for in-camp publications.

In Amache, as in the nine other relocation camps, a cooperative handled most consumer services. The Amache Consumer's Cooperative, owned and operated by the evacuees, was established in 1943. WRA policy not only authorized such associations but prohibited the establishment of any other kind of consumer services, causing *Fortune* magazine to comment that the WRA was forbidding individual enterprise within the camps.[20] This policy appears to have been linked not only to the WRA's emphasis on relocation outside the camp, but also to anxieties regarding the maintenance of uniform wages in the camps,[21] a source of controversy among anti-Japanese forces. Barbers, clerks, and other cooperative workers all received a standard stipend according to the low WRA wage scale under which professionals received $19 a month, skilled workers were paid $16, and the unskilled $12. The Amache cooperative was supervised by a board of directors and several committees elected from among the 2,650 members. The cooperative stores and shops, housed in a U-shaped building composed of three barracks, offered clothing, shoes, and shoe repairs. In addition, there was a barber shop and beauty parlor, a canteen, a newspaper department, and a cleaning-and-pressing service.

Agriculture became the largest of the Amache enterprises. Early on, the WRA had determined that the evacuees should grow as much of their own food as possible and in that way assist in keeping camp menus to the ration cost of not more than 45 cents per person daily. Consequently, all of the camps grew vegetables and raised hogs. According to the report of a Euro-American staff officer, the Amache farm program had two main objectives: to produce as much of the crops and livestock needed to feed the evacuees and to "provide physical and mental employment acceptable to the residents."[22]

The federal government had acquired the sprawling 10,221.92 acres of the Granada project — another name for the Amache Relocation Center area — from private owners by direct purchase or condemnation. The camp center, the location of the administration buildings and barracks, occupied 640 of these acres. The two largest pieces of land were gained by condemnation: The biggest piece comprised 4,688 acres owned by Elbert S.

Rule; the second largest piece — 3,712 acres known as the Koen Ranch — was bought from the American Crystal Sugar Company.[23] Some of this land had been used for pasture but no one had ever before tried to grow vegetables on it.

In this agricultural endeavor, the camp supplied evacuee labor and supervisors; the government provided water, equipment, seed, and technical personnel. Initially, the technical staff consisted of four men and later, six: a chief of agriculture, a farm superintendent, two assistant superintendents, and two labor foremen. The farmland and various enterprises such as vegetable production, livestock, and food preserving were divided into a number of operating units, each headed by a Japanese American supervisor.[24] The agricultural section operated through 1943 and 1944. Although vegetable cultivation ceased in 1945, meat production continued until the closing of the center on October 15, 1945.

The evacuees grew a variety of crops that ranged from produce such as mung bean sprouts, daikon (Japanese radish), celery, lettuce, tomatoes and tea to feed crops like alfalfa, corn, sorghum, and milo. In all, the Amache farm yielded 6,051,661 pounds of vegetables grown on 1,044 acres, as well as 1,237,463 pounds of pork and beef, of which 285,230 pounds were sold to the highest bidder and to the Denver Livestock Commission companies. About one-fourth of the feed crops grown for Amache livestock was sold to the public as surplus. Despite the initial problems of inadequate machinery and facilities, and the internees' unfamiliarity with the Colorado terrain, the Amache farm produced enough of a surplus to ship some produce to other relocation centers.

As the Euro-American staff officer observed in his report, the farm project faced "numerous problems distinctly peculiar to the unusual circumstances under which it was conceived." One of these problems involved the lack of facilities: The poultry unit had 8,000 laying hens and housing for only 3,000; this resulted in feeding difficulties and low egg production, as hens laid eggs in an open twenty-acre field. Similarly, the hog project lacked enough pens for the segregation of new pigs and was also troubled by severe epidemics. Hundreds of acres of grain and corn were lost to drought because of irrigation problems.

Labor supply, however, proved to be the most crucial problem of the Amache farm program. Soon after the farm operations started, the WRA began issuing short-term leave permits to internees. Many, especially the Nisei, anxiously desired to escape the confines of camp and to seek higher wages than the standard $16 per month offered to relocation camp farm workers. Although both women and men left, most of those who did temporary agricultural work were male. Given the wartime labor shortage, many farmers were eager to have Japanese American workers, and as the staff officer ruefully noted, this placed the camp in competition with the labor demand on the outside. "It was not unusual for the [Amache] farm to lose all of its tractor drivers over night or to have 25–50% of its trained supervisors leave within a period of two weeks. . . . When, in the spring of 1944, 29 of the 42 farm supervisors left, it created a problem little short of tragic."[25]

The staff officer's report reveals not only the patronizing attitude of government administrators but also the evacuees' resistance to low-paid camp labor and their determination to act in their own interest. Not all could be described as willing docile workers in the relocation camp. Anger and frustration led some to say, "The government brot me here. They will have to feed me. I no work."[26] The most "loyal and willing workers," the officer found, were the Issei men and women — coincidentally those least likely to be able to leave the camps in search of temporary work elsewhere. The staff officer's approval of their willingness suggested mixed motives. He lauded the effort of hundreds of Japanese American volunteers who took time from their regular nonagricultural jobs to help with the harvest, but qualified his praise: "Too many wanted to work in the melon patch and some of the crops such as sweet potatoes, pop corn, daikon and beans made poor recorded yields because the volunteers carried home a large percentage of the crop they harvested."[27]

In addition, workers sought to exert some control over the pace of their labor. For instance, workers on the Koen Ranch section ate lunch at a mess hall established in the old Koen Hotel at the center of the farm. From the administrators' point of view, this practice "discouraged the tendency for workers to remain home in the afternoons," but it also allowed some workers to "sit under the shade for two hours each day."[28]

Despite the talk of common effort and self-sustenance, the hard fact remained that the evacuees performed arduous labor for poor wages, and the crops they produced did not mean individual bonuses or improvements. Little wonder, then, that many seized the opportunity to leave in search of better "physical and mental employment." And in light of the working and living conditions in the camp, the personal reaping of melons and daikon can be seen as a small means of resistance, individual and peer sanctioned. Securing a few hours of rest in the shade meant exercising a fraction of control and choice, which in turn provided a minimal basis of self-esteem.

The conditions of work and life in the relocation center necessitated flexibility. Like the Merced Assembly Center, the Amache Camp brought together a diverse group of people, young and old, urban and rural. Although most Cortez interviewees recalled that everyone had gotten along "pretty well," it is useful to balance these memories with evidence from the past that can illuminate details ordinarily filtered out by time. The massing together of so many different people in a small camp sparked strong reactions from some of the youth, whose letters indicate that harmonious relations did not come easily or quickly. Many adjustments had to be made. For example, urban-rural tensions erupted often in the early months. One Livingston teenager wrote to a former teacher, describing the animosity between the "Livingstonians" and "Santa Anitans": "I wish we could get unity here but it seems an impossible situation. If one from L.A. gets a grudge against a certain country person, they get in a big gang of fifteen or so and just knock the dickens out of this *one* person." She went on to detail the differences in urban Nisei fashion, which astonished some of the rural onlookers: "They carry knives, too, and are proud of it. They also wear zoot suits* (pleated at the cuffs of the pants legs) and long ¾ length coat-jackets — really disgusting." [29]

Two other high school students, one from Cortez and the other from Livingston, also complained of the rowdy behavior of the Santa Anita and Tanforan Nisei who were "always fighting or making trouble for us" at camp dances. "We don't get along with them," one concluded, "because they're city slickers and we're mostly country hicks." [30] These conflicts at Amache also exemplify some of the internal dissension that arose from regional loyalties at the various camps, each of which, according to Girdner and Loftis, "had its own atmosphere, dependent on the previous experience of evacuees there." [31]

A concern common to all the centers in the eyes of administrators, scholars, and inmates was the effect of camp life on the family. Nisei sociologist Harry Kitano, interned at the Topaz Camp, has asserted that in general, "the evacuation tended toward the destruction of established family patterns of behavior." [32] Daisuke Kitagawa, a Christian Issei minister at Tule Lake, similarly reported the breakdown of traditional functions and the sense of family unity in the artificial community. [33] Both agreed that this brought about significant change in individual roles and expectations.

Notable alterations occurred in gender dynamics, with corresponding changes in family relations. A number of Issei women, accustomed to long days of work inside and outside the home, found that communally prepared meals and limited living quarters provided them with spare time. Although some experienced disorientation, many availed themselves of the opportunity to enjoy the company of their female peers and to attend adult classes ranging from handicrafts and Japanese arts to English. [34]

While these women gained an increased measure of independence, Kitano and Kitagawa observed, Issei men faced the loss of the authority and

---

zoot suit: a style of men's clothing, characterized by a flamboyant long jacket, baggy pegged pants, a long key chain, and shoes with thick soles, that was popular among rebellious young men in the 1940s.

responsibility to which they were accustomed. No longer the major bread-winners of the family, they might in some cases be earning the same wages as their wives and children. And no matter how hard the Issei man worked, Kitagawa stated, "he could not improve the living conditions of his family."[35] The Issei men also lost much of their control of community leadership, because their alien status barred them from political activity under WRA rulings. These blows, as Jeanne Wakatsuki Houston recorded in her autobiographical account, *Farewell to Manzanar,* contributed to the deterioration of morale suffered by a number of the first generation.

A major anxiety of Issei parents and the older Nisei concerned the effect of the camp environment on the younger Nisei. In the relocation centers, the federal government assumed the family's function of providing food, clothing, and shelter, which in conjunction with the physical conditions loosened the reins of family social control.[36] In 1944, Leonard Bloom reported that the peer group had replaced the family as the organizing principle, and that the arrangement of community activities along age lines reinforced this tendency. Consequently, he asserted, each family member had become a "free agent," and "children detached themselves from parental supervision, returning to the home barracks perhaps only to sleep."[37] One worried parent at Tule Lake, Professor Yamato Ishihashi, lamented the "stealing out of stores and homes, smart alec thievery which we never had among Japanese children," and declared, "We no longer control our own families."[38]

A Nisei who voiced similar concerns was Eddie Shimano, editor first of the Santa Anita center newsletter and then of the *Communique* of the relocation camp at Jerome, Arkansas. He later served with the all-Nisei 442nd Regimental Combat Team. In an article published in the liberal journal *Common Ground* in 1943, Shimano indicted the camp's work system and its education courses, but he leveled his harshest critique at the effect of camp conditions on the Japanese American youth, who, "somewhere in the evacuation . . . had lost their pride." Genevieve Carter, a psychologist at Manzanar, echoed this concern over the fear and insecurity of adolescent Nisei regarding their place in a hostile society that denied their rights as citizens.[39] Shimano particularly noted how, as a substitute for lost pride and sense of belonging, many young men from their late teens to mid-twenties had formed "pachuco gangs"* in the camps. These youths were emulated by the younger boys, who formed "junior gangs." Shimano observed, in accordance with the Cortez and Livingston teenagers, that "The pachuco gangs, easily spotted . . . by their 'uniforms' and long haircuts and zoot suits, crash

---

pachuco gang: a group of Mexican American youths who often wore zoot suits and spoke Calo, an inventive mixture of English and Spanish.

social affairs, settle all personal grudges with physical assault, and follow pretty closely the pattern set by the Dead End gangs."*[40] There are certainly parallels between the second-generation Mexican American youth of Los Angeles who, facing an "iron curtain" of discrimination, turned to close-knit peer groups for security and status, and those Nisei teenagers who, branded as enemy aliens by fellow Americans and conscious of their parents' vulnerability, banded together in the camps.[41] Journalist Carey McWilliams's interpretation of the pachucos' zoot suits as "at once a sign of rebellion and a mark of belonging" can be extended to the Nisei's style of dress.[42]

At Amache, a number of Cortez Issei parents had cause to lament the influence of gangs and the wild behavior of their sons. (They hardly imagined their children's eventual respectability within the community.) One group of boys organized to counter the forays of the Los Angeles gangs, under the leadership of a very young Cortez teenager, Takeshi Sugiura, still known today as "General."

In the camps, where individuals spent most of their time with companions of their own age and gender, peer pressure could exert enormous force. For some, groups did provide a sense of camaraderie, but for others, gangs and peer pressure left lingering scars. One Cortez Nisei still remembers with pain the humiliation of being forced to shoplift items from the canteen for the older boys.

The majority of teenagers and children did not participate in gangs and violence. Many found outlets for their energies in sports, cultural events, and religious groups. Some, like Howard Taniguchi, took part in dramatic productions. Others, like Yuri Yamamoto and her siblings, were very much involved in Christian Endeavor activities. Like the assembly center, the camp offered a variety of classes and activities. However, this was not "summer camp." The dark side of internment shadowed the lives of the Nisei and provided yet another impetus for those who wished to leave.

Regardless of age and activities, the Nisei were highly conscious of their separation from "life on the outside," and their banishment to somewhere that wasn't quite America to them. This awareness—whether angry, wistful, or bewildered—permeated their wartime writings. In this vein the 1944 Amache High School yearbook was dedicated to the Japanese American soldiers: "our brothers, our friends, our schoolmates, and our heroes—who will be 'over there' fighting for those ideals that they believe in and wish to establish and maintain for us." The yearbook was titled the *1944 Onlooker,* implying that "we are onlookers—of necessity" but also looking to the future with the hope of "being once again within the orbit of world affairs."[43]

---

*Dead End gang: a group of tough neighborhood kids; the term became popular after the 1937 movie *Dead End,* which featured a gang of delinquents from New York City's East Side slum.

A Nisei woman soon to leave Amache expressed some of the evacuees' ambivalent feelings in a "love letter" to America, included at the end of the yearbook. The letter was dated April 30, 1944, two years from the very day "I ceased to be a part of you [America]." She found:

> The new surroundings and experiences occupied all my attention at first, and my loneliness for you was crowded out. . . . I crammed my hours with continuous activity so that there would not be a chance for that loneliness to enter my being and begin its steady flow through my veins.

Like other evacuees, she discovered that "This plan worked wonderfully at first, but the activities soon became a drudgery to me." She also wrote obliquely of the injustice of evacuation:

> I worship you in spite of the errors you have made. Yes, you have made errors and you have roamed on many wrong roads; but everyone makes mistakes. . . . All I ask is that you do not make the same mistake twice; that is inexcusable even in the eyes of one who loves you so.

She concluded her letter with the anticipation of her approaching return to life on the outside. "I hope that your faith in me has grown since the last time I saw you," she wrote in quiet challenge, for "that faith must grow for my faith in you to grow."[44] Many Nisei carried such hopes with them to the Midwest and East when they left the isolated world of the camp, unsure of their reception but eager to return to America.

The machinery of their return moved slowly. The WRA's leave-clearance procedures and resettlement policy evolved cumbrously in the first two years of internment. The first to leave the camps in 1942 were workers with temporary leave permits. Because of the complicated screening process, few besides college students departed on "indefinite leave." In 1943 the WRA tried to expedite the clearance procedure by broadening an army registration program, aimed at Nisei males, to include all adults. With this policy change — and despite some tragic consequences, including postwar expatriation — an increasing stream of Japanese Americans, mostly Nisei, left the camps to seek work and education, or to go off to war.[45]

In 1942 the WRA began to release temporarily Japanese Americans from assembly centers and relocation camps to do voluntary farmwork in neighboring areas hard hit by the wartime labor shortage. There was a particular demand for sugar-beet workers in Colorado. "During the harvest season a lot of farmers came into the camp to get the workers," recalled Kumekichi Taniguchi. "We went, too. We got stung."[46] After Kumekichi and a group of workers finished a back-breaking stint of beet-topping at one place, the farmer refused to pay them. Kumekichi's experience was not an unusual one. Vulnerable to exploitation, the evacuees had no real recourse to reimbursement when cheated. Their work conditions varied from situation to situation and from region to region, depending largely on the integrity of the individual farmer.

Despite their being credited with saving the sugar-beet crop of Utah, Idaho, Montana, and Wyoming, and having harvested much of Arizona's staple cotton crop, the Japanese Americans were not well received in all regions.[47] When the WRA began issuing "indefinite leave" permits, it directed the evacuees to the Midwest and East and also had to launch a public relations campaign, as Weglyn explained, "not only to mitigate evacuee fears but also to reeducate a paranoiac public to differentiate between the bitterly despised foes across the Pacific and fellow U.S. citizens."[48] A number of religious groups and service organizations — such as the American Friends Service Committee — provided invaluable aid in resettling internees.

By the fall of 1942, the likelihood of a Japanese attack on the United States had faded before Allied victories in the Pacific and, with it, the military justification for the internment of the Japanese Americans. How the WRA should proceed became the subject of complicated wrangling among civilian and army leaders.[49] The debate over whether the Nisei — then classified as enemy aliens — should be allowed to enlist in the armed forces soon meshed with the larger issue of the evacuees' return to normal life. The decision to probe their loyalty meant agonizing choices for many of the interned. As the Commission on Wartime Relocation and Internment of Civilians stated forty years later, "It is a bitter irony that the loyalty review program, which the WRA and the War Department established as the predicate for release from the camps — the first major decision in which the interests of the evacuees prevailed — was carried out without sufficient sensitivity or knowledge of the evacuees. Designed to hasten their release, the program instead became one of the most divisive, wrenching episodes of the captivity."[50]

In early 1943 army officers began to administer a questionnaire designed to determine the background and loyalties of the Nisei men; the WRA also prepared an "Application for Leave Clearance" geared to the Issei and the Nisei women. The distribution of these questionnaires to all evacuees over the age of seventeen resulted in a brutal streamlining of the clearance process. Elderly men and women, who were barred from naturalization, and American-born Nisei, who had been denied the rights of citizenship — all of whom had been recently torn from homes, businesses, and communities — were now expected to affirm their allegiance to the United States. This meant forswearing loyalty to any other country, as well as testifying to their willingness to serve in the armed forces of the country that had imprisoned them. This "colossal folly" became further compounded by the combining of the mass registration with an army recruitment drive which, as Weglyn pointed out, evidenced the restoration of one right: "the right to be shot at."[51]

The loyalty oath and army registration issue created painful dissension within many families, often between parents and sons, especially in the California and Arizona camps, which were surrounded by strong public hostility. Despite the internal conflicts, many Nisei men registered, eager to demonstrate their loyalty and willing to pay with their blood for acknowledgment as Americans. Just as registration required courage, so did the decision not to register. One Cortez Nisei who refused to go for an induction physical when called for duty by the Selective Service challenged the authorities: "If you were an able-bodied person in my situation, what would you do?" The answer was a six-month sentence in federal prison.[52]

Other Cortez Nisei — including Hiroshi Asai, Key Kobayashi, Kaoru Masuda, Ken Miyamoto, Howard Taniguchi, and Kiyoshi Yamamoto — joined the approximately 33,000 Japanese Americans, half from Hawaii and half from the mainland, who fought in World War II.[53] Like many Nisei men, they served in the highly acclaimed 442nd Regimental Combat Team and with military intelligence after receiving training at the Military Intelligence Service Language School, which graduated nearly 6,000 Nisei by the end of the war. Nisei women served as well: more than 200 joined the U.S. Cadet Nursing Corps and some 100 entered the Women's Army Corps, including 51 linguists trained as translators by the Military Intelligence Service Language School at Fort Snelling.[54]

Of the Japanese American men and women who served in many capacities during World War II, the best known are the 100th Infantry Battalion and the 442nd Regimental Combat Team who together became known as "The Purple Heart Regiment" for the allegiance they proved in blood. Their motto, "Go for broke," was a Hawaiian gambler's expression, and their emblem — chosen in preference to the War Department's original design of a yellow arm grasping a red sword — was a silver hand bearing a torch, on a field of blue. By the end of the war, they had garnered 18,143 individual awards for valor, becoming "the most decorated unit for its size and length of service in the history of the United States."[55]

The 100th Battalion had its inception in a recommendation by Hawaiian Commander Lieutenant General Delos Emmons. In February 1942, upon learning that the Department of War intended to release the Nisei from active duty, Emmons — mindful of both the Hawaiian Japanese Americans' wish to participate in military service and their role in the local workforce — suggested the formation of a Nisei unit. After more than a year of training on the mainland, the initial 1,432 men of the 100th Battalion arrived in North Africa in September 1943. They sustained heavy casualties and earned 900 Purple Hearts in the grueling Allied campaign through Italy.[56]

The 100th Battalion soon met with the 442nd Regimental Combat Team in the offensive from the Anzio beachhead in June 1944. Comprised principally of Hawaiian and mainland Nisei, the 442nd had trained primarily at Camp Shelby in Mississippi from October 1943 to February 1944. The 100th Battalion formally became part of the 442nd on June 15, 1944.[57] The officers of both the 100th and the 442nd were predominantly Euro-Americans, but all of the enlisted men were Nisei, classified by their draft boards as "4-C, Enemy Alien."

Hiro Asai, one of the Cortez Nisei who served in the 442nd, joined in 1943, went to a training camp in Florida and then to Fort Meade, Maryland. He reached France with the 442nd in the winter of 1944. They stayed at Brest, on the Atlantic Coast of Normandy, holding the line until more replacements arrived; then they received orders to ship out to Italy. They fought all the way up northern Italy, from Leghorn to near Genoa. The day before the war ended in Italy, Hiro was wounded by a hand grenade: "We were fighting from hill to hill . . . up in the mountains. . . . We were advancing so fast that they told us to hold the line until the rest of the Allied Forces could come up in line, because there would be too much of a gap." The commanding officer wanted to press on, but contented himself with sending a scouting force—Hiro's platoon—ahead to gauge enemy resistance. When they reached the "next hill" several miles away, "all hell broke loose. They started shooting us from all sides and from behind, too." Six of the platoon were wounded, but all escaped.[58]

The 100th and the 442nd fought in seven major campaigns in France and Italy, including the famed rescue of the "Lost Battalion." Ordered to reach at any cost the 211 survivors of the 141st Regiment, surrounded by Germans near Bruyères, the 442nd did so with a sacrifice of more than 200 dead and 600 wounded. By the end of the war, the 100th and the 442nd had suffered 9,486 casualties, "more than twice the assigned complement of men in the unit."[59] The exploits of the 442nd and the 100th attracted much public attention in the United States and, in the words of writer Noriko Sawada Bridges, made them "Our stepping stones to freedom."[60]

The Nisei who graduated from the Military Intelligence Service Language School (MISLS) and served in nonsegregated units in the Pacific have received less recognition, despite the critical role they played as translators, interpreters, interrogators, and cave-flushers. Major General Charles Willoughby, MacArthur's chief of intelligence, claimed that "the Nisei MIS shortened the Pacific war by two years."[61] Their activities long remained a military secret, partly for their own protection, partly to conceal from the enemy the existence of expert linguists who were translating intercepted materials and questioning prisoners.[62] Joseph D. Harrington has contended that "a grudging Pentagon" kept silent about the details of their service for three decades after the war.[63]

The MISLS, according to Masaharu Ano, was the only source of linguists for the U.S. military during World War II. The school opened in November 1941 at the Presidio in San Francisco; there the students immersed themselves in intensive study of spoken and written Japanese, document analysis and interrogation, as well as Japanese geography, culture, and military structure. In June 1942 the program moved to Camp Savage in Minnesota, spurred both by the need for larger facilities and by public hostility toward the specially recruited Nisei students. Rapid growth prompted another move to Fort Snelling, Minnesota, where the program remained until it found a permanent base in 1946 at the Presidio in Monterey, California.[64] The first MISLS graduates met with suspicion by military officers who balked at accepting them. This changed, however, after they proved their loyalty and skill in the Aleutian Islands and at Guadalcanal.[65] More than 5,000 MISLS graduates, the large majority of them Nisei, served with 130 different units of the armed forces and on loan to Allied armies.[66] After the war, they became a "language bridge" between the Allied occupation forces and the Japanese, working as translators at war crimes trials, gathering statistics for an Atomic Bomb Survey, and acting as censors.[67]

Among the highly trained MISLS graduates was Kiyoshi Yamamoto, a Cortez Nisei. Kiyoshi had finished his last year of high school in Amache and then, after discovering resistance from some state universities toward Japanese American students, he attended, like many Nisei, a church-affiliated school. After a year of studying engineering in Iowa, he received his draft notice. "I thought, 'Well, there's an opportunity to go to the language school and go to the Pacific.'" Kiyoshi passed the qualifying exam and went to the MISLS — first at Camp Savage and then Fort Snelling — for nine months of rigorous training in Japanese. "We had intensive schooling from eight to four during the day, and compulsory studies from seven to nine. We were required to go from seven to nine, but most of us studied from six to ten, so we really studied hard."[68] The MISLS teachers were all Japanese Americans — some Kibei (Nisei sent to Japan for education and then repatriated) and some Nisei — as were all of the students.

Inequities persisted at the MISLS as in other branches of the army. Kiyoshi noted that at Fort Snelling there was also "an officers' candidate school . . . and it was all *hakujin* [white people] taking Japanese. But when they graduated, they were officers. When we graduated, we were just enlisted men. . . . All we got was a few stripes."[69] Harrington reached a similar verdict, stating, "Nisei got an unfair deal regarding advancement during the war although 100 or so were commissioned in 1945 as a public relations ploy. Very few got commissions before then. . . . Despite their colossal combined achievements, few Nisei ended the war higher than Staff Sergeant, and most finished at a lower grade."[70]

After Kiyoshi had completed nine months of language studies and two months of basic training, the war with Japan ended when atomic bombs were dropped on Hiroshima and Nagasaki. "So they rushed us — we went to the Philippines first and then from the Philippines some of the boys went to the war crimes trial in Manila; some went to the signing of the peace on the *Missouri;* and some went to the war crimes trial in Tokyo."[71] Kiyoshi was sent to Tokyo where he interrogated Japanese Air Force officers and translated the index of an air force manual. During his tour of duty, he traveled in Japan and met his parents' relatives in Yamaguchi-ken: "It was a strange feeling, because they felt strange, too. They knew I was their nephew, yet serving in the occupational forces. They couldn't quite understand. But it was nice. I went to visit them twice."[72]

While Nisei like Kiyoshi Yamamoto and Hiro Asai departed from the camps to serve in the armed forces, others left the barbed wire perimeters to face new challenges on the home front.

College students were the first to depart from the camps with indefinite leave permits. Between 1942 and 1946, 4,084 of them did so with the assistance of the National Japanese American Student Relocation Council, a nongovernmental agency largely composed of concerned educators.[73] The NJASRC proved instrumental in persuading schools outside the Western Defense Zone to accept Japanese American students and helping them to obtain leave clearances.

Some of the students had graduated from the makeshift high schools set up in the camps; others were trying to continue a college education abruptly terminated by the evacuation. In 1941, on the eve of the war, 3,530 Nisei were attending college.[74] Mark Kamiya had completed one year of agricultural studies when the war began. While doing temporary work outside the Amache camp — washing, sacking, and loading potatoes and working in fields of sugar beets and cantaloupes — he began to apply for college admission. The first to accept him was Brigham Young University, but he found the racial attitudes prevailing there incompatible with his own. After taking a required course in religion in which the professor expounded on the inferiority of African Americans, Mark could stand it no longer. Three quarters after his arrival, he left. He then went to Cornell University, known for its fine agricultural department, to see if the college would accept him. Cornell denied him admission, first on the grounds that they preferred not to take out-of-state students. Mark knew that the school was practically empty. He finally asked a university administrator, "Isn't it because I'm Japanese that you don't want to accept me?" The man admitted it was true, and then said, "Well, after talking to you, I think we can accept you for one semester."[75] In anticipation, Mark took a job in a local dairy, but discovered during his eight months there that he wanted to study Hegel and Marx rather than crop rotation. After the war and his completion of an eighteen-month tour of duty in the army, he enrolled in the University of California at Berkeley and graduated with a degree in philosophy.

Nisei women comprised an unprecedented 40 percent of the relocating college students.[76] According to the U.S. Census of 1940, women constituted 32 percent of the 1,132 Nisei over the age of twenty-five who had completed one to three years of college, and 29 percent of the 1,049 who had four or more years. Among them was Mary Noda, who finished high school in Amache and then attended Colorado State University at Greeley for two years. It was her "first time away from home," and like many other students, she worried about the transition to college. "I was worried about my ability to do the work. . . . I worried so much I couldn't study."[77] The strain of adjustment to the university and life away from her family was compounded by a taxing schedule of domestic work that helped pay for her education.

Despite their uncertainties about the reception awaiting them and several early incidents of hostility, the Nisei continued to leave for schools, many in areas where they became the first Asian Americans ever seen. The previous presence of Japanese Americans in an area, however, did not necessarily make the adjustment any easier. The Japanese Americans in Colorado were among the fortunate minority who lived outside the military defense zone on the West Coast, and so escaped internment. As one Cortez Nisei remembered painfully, some of the Colorado college instructors compared the evacuated California students unfavorably with the uninterned Nisei with whom they were familiar and demanded, "Why aren't you like the Colorado Japanese?" The differences in economic concerns, clothes, poise, and self-confidence were obvious, but any answer to that insensitive question would have been painful and unspeakable during the war years.

By 1943, as the WRA's resettlement program developed, increasing numbers of Japanese Americans streamed from the relocation camps to the Midwest and East. By August 1943, almost 11,000 evacuees had left the camps on indefinite leave and by the end of 1944, approximately 35,000 — or a third of the original camp population — had gone.[78] These included predominantly single Nisei and young couples whose language skills, citizenship, and age gave them a better chance than the Issei in the labor market. Among them were a large number of women; as Leonard Bloom noted, "Japanese traditions of control over young women failed to materially affect their relocation rate."[79] Women's developing sense of independence in the camp environment and their growing awareness of their abilities as workers contributed to their self-confidence and hence their desire to leave. By the end of the war, 37 percent of the evacuees sixteen years or older had already relocated, including 63 percent of the Nisei women in that age group.[80]

Because job availability and general reception of the Japanese Americans were better in urban centers than in rural areas, most headed for the cities. Accordingly, the WRA established field offices in Chicago, Cleveland, Denver, Kansas City, Little Rock, New York, and Salt Lake City.[81] There, with the placement assistance of the WRA and various religious and service organizations, the Japanese Americans turned their energies to adjusting to life in new environments.

Although they found work in restaurants, factories, and businesses, the most numerous job requests for Japanese American women and men were in the field of domestic service. As the wartime labor shortage opened new doors for African American, Mexican American, and Euro-American women, many of them left domestic positions for better-paying work in factories and defense plants. Nisei like Yeichi and May Sakaguchi and Miye Kato filled the open positions.

Like many Japanese Americans who traveled with friends or kin, Miye Kato left Amache in September, 1943, with three other Nisei — June Taniguchi, Takako Hashimoto, and Sumi Nishihara. Miye found a domestic job in Medford, Connecticut, through a Methodist church. Two of the ministers had visited Amache and subsequently helped to relocate the Japanese Americans. "They looked after us and whenever we had free time, they would invite us over to their home. If we had any problem, we asked them."[82] June worked with Miye's sister in a girls' dormitory in Bridgeport, Connecticut, and soon Miye obtained a position with a lawyer's family there.

After a year in Bridgeport, Miye and her sister decided to go to Chicago. She recounted: "We tried hotel work, but we lasted only one day! We didn't like it at all. So we went again to find a domestic job." From Chicago they moved to Evanston, Illinois, to be closer to their brother who was stationed at Camp Savage in Minnesota. There they found work situations with families who treated them well; and there Miye stayed until her marriage to Nobuzo Baba at Amache in July 1945.[83]

While some Nisei found mutual support in journeying forth together, others ventured alone into regions where few, if any, Japanese Americans had ever traveled. After she spent two years at Greeley, Mary Noda's brother — then a teacher in Iowa — helped her find a position in North Dakota. There, at age nineteen, she taught strapping seventh- and eighth-graders in a town of 200. "It was a nice experience," she recalled. "They had never seen a Japanese American." The superintendent had been too afraid to tell anyone that the new teacher was Japanese American, but tried to mitigate the surprise by saying, "I don't know what's coming. She might be an Indian." In fact, Mary said, "People thought I was an Indian on the train." During her year in North Dakota, Mary boarded with a Russian-German immigrant woman and grew accustomed to eating meat, white bread, and potatoes three times a day. The townspeople invited her to stay on, but she returned to California in 1946 to finish her education degree at San Francisco State University.[84]

Many men and a lesser number of women — like Florice Kuwahara and Ruth Nishi Yoshida — found jobs as factory workers. Florice and Sam Kuwahara left Amache in May 1943 to work on a farm in Adams City, Colorado. After one painful week — "Whatever I earned, I was spending on liniment," recalled Sam — they moved to Denver. There Sam worked in the produce business and Florice took a job doing piecework in a garment factory. "I don't know how much they paid us, I think it was about 25 cents an hour, but by the time they took my income tax, my Social Security, and war bonds, there wasn't much left." Florice laughed and added, "Of course, that was when I just started. . . . But everything was cheap in those days."[85] Florice worked there for three years, a long record among the Nisei during the war.

Because of the varying work conditions and wages, job turnover among the Nisei was high. Ernest Yoshida's wartime work history illustrates this trend. Admitted to the Milwaukee School of Engineering in the fall of 1942, he arrived on campus only to find that most of the instructors had been drafted, and no one could teach the courses he wanted to take. The school refused to refund his tuition payment and told him he could take classes in welding, a skill he already had. Ernest encountered another Nisei in the same situation, Tad Morishige (whose cousin knew Ernie), and together they went to Chicago to seek work. On their first night there, on a lead from their landlady, they began work as stockboys at a soda-water bottling plant, for $1.82 an hour. A short time later, they found work at the Cuneo Press which printed *Time* magazine and *Newsweek*. There for six months Ernest was assistant to a "trimmer" who trimmed the sides of the magazine. Then the two Nisei began making pup-tent valves at a factory where Ernie met his future wife, Ruth Nishi. For a short time he installed radios in army jeeps, but the cold, dark workplace motivated him to apply elsewhere. After three weeks as a bottler for Canadian Club, a blended whiskey, Ernest went to a house-trailer factory where he could use his skills as a carpenter. The piece-work payment was excellent but the management's treatment deplorable. One day, a janitor's accidental push caused Ernest to lose part of a finger to a wood router from which the safety guard had been removed for the sake of speed. The boss said he was "too busy" to take him to a doctor, so, bleeding profusely, Ernest had to find a streetcar. When he quit the job, two other angry Nisei left with him.[86]

According to Hosokawa and Wilson, "The first evacuees to be hired by a firm were often the best argument for hiring additional evacuees."[87] They were not only the best argument, but also frequently the means of hiring the additional evacuees. After George Yuge found a job making ammunition boxes at a Denver defense plant, the boss, impressed by the crate-nailing skills that he developed in Cortez, asked, "Do you know any other Japanese who can do that?" "I know a few," George said, and soon Smile Kamiya and five other Nisei were hard at work hammering together boxes with him.[88]

In the midst of their travels and job hunting, like earlier groups of working-class rural migrants and foreign immigrants, the Japanese Americans relied upon a flexible support network of friends and relatives, otherwise known as chain migration. Many of them combined forces in the search for jobs and lodging, like Ernest and Tad. Their ties to associates from their former communities and the camps formed vital grapevines, passing news of work and hospitable neighborhoods as well as warnings of exploitative situations. News traveled quickly, as Ernest learned at his next job at the Fowler McCormick tractor assembly plant. After a week of sweeping the floor, he was put on the line for small tractors. Two days later, a manager promoted him to the position of line foreman and asked him to find some more Japanese Americans to work on the line. Ernest told Brush Arai, a Hawaiian friend, that he needed fifty people right away. In a week, fifty arrived from three camps: Amache, Rohwer Camp in Arkansas, and Heart Mountain Camp, Wyoming. To the delight of the management, tractor production increased from 74 to 86 on their first day of work, and within three months they had increased the production to 136 tractors a day.[89]

The Japanese Americans who resettled first not only passed along information but also provided way stations for the friends and relatives who followed. When George and Helen Yuge left the Poston Camp for Denver, they lived with Helen's father and mother-in-law, Helen's sister and brother, George's brother, Smile Kamiya, and another Nisei who later died in Italy serving with the 442nd. "It used to be like a boardinghouse." When Helen and George moved to their own home in a different part of town, one of Helen's nieces lived with them, as well as several other people. "And every Saturday night, never missed, there used to be great big poker parties," George recalled.

> I never played poker at home [before the war], but the fellows there would come, and she'd always have a big dinner for them. . . . All these Nisei GIs on furlough would congregate down at our place. Many of them we knew—they were all kids from Watsonville and Salinas and places like that. They didn't have any place to go, so they'd come over, or a friend would bring a friend. . . . Gosh, it was nothing Saturday night to have eighteen, twenty people sitting there.[90]

Although they often worked with *hakujin,* the Nisei generally socialized with other Nisei. It was their ties to Japanese American friends and family on which they drew for emotional support and understanding during the war years.

It is impossible to summarize neatly the wartime experiences and feelings of even one family or community, much less the entire Japanese American population. A small number, living beyond the Western Defense Zone, were not evacuated, but 120,000 in the zone were: some to prison camps, the majority to ten concentration camps or "relocation centers." Of these, Wilson and Hosokawa have stated, "It can be safely said that there were no happy Relocation Centers. All had their problems."[91] The Issei and Nisei did their best to make that life as bearable and regular as possible, and a large number of them — both women and men — left it as soon as they could.

Regardless of the length of their stay in the camps, all were affected by the evacuation. In addition to economic and psychological losses, internment altered family roles and accelerated the trends that differentiated the second generation from their parents. Kitano has emphasized the impact of evacuation and relocation on the acculturation of the Japanese Americans: "New exposure, new opportunities, the dissolution of old institutions and structures, and life away from the ghetto hastened change."[92] While the structure of camp life loosened parental control of children, the WRA policies transferred community leadership from the Issei to the Nisei, resulting, as several scholars have contended, in competition between the two generations and the increasing independence of the Nisei.

In addition to generational roles, as Kitagawa and others have observed, gender roles also changed. As before the war, most family members worked, but men, women, boys, and girls all received the same low wage, which increased the independence of women. Furthermore, when the relocation program began, Nisei women as well as men traveled far from their families to seek opportunities in the Midwest and East.[93]

The experiences of the Cortez people reflect the stress and hardship of camp and relocation. However, the patterns of their lives also evidence the strength of support networks formed before and during the war, and the continuity of ties of affection and responsibility. Whether they departed for military service or to pursue jobs and education, all faced adjustment to unfamiliar environments and work. They were sustained through this period by deep-rooted networks of relatives and friends, and they maintained family bonds even though many journeyed farther from home than ever before. It was a time of independence, camaraderie, and experimentation as well as frustration, insecurity, and loneliness.

By 1945, 35,000 Japanese Americans had already resettled outside the Western Defense Zone. After the War Department ended the exclusion of the Japanese Americans from the West Coast, the majority chose to return. Many individuals and families journeyed back to the areas they called "home," but the available evidence indicates that Cortez, Cressey, and Livingston are the only communities that returned *as communities,* in an organized fashion. The hardship of rebuilding and the salvaging of dreams that awaited them would prove as demanding of their resources and stamina as the initial evacuation. The new Cortez would be a different one, the structure and contours of its relationships altered by the transfer of leadership to the Nisei, the influx of newcomers — mostly women marrying into the community — and the arrival of the Sansei, the third generation.

Notes

1. Henry Kusaba, James C. Lindley, and Joe McClelland, *Amache,* a report (Amache, Colo.: Documentation Section, Reports Office, ca. 1944).

2. Robert A. Wilson and Bill Hosokawa, *East to America: A History of the Japanese in the United States* (New York: William Morrow and Company, 1980), pp. 212–13. The Poston and Manzanar camps were begun as assembly centers by the U.S. Army.

3. Dillon S. Myer, *Uprooted Americans: The Japanese Americans and the War Relocation Authority during World War II* (Tucson: University of Arizona Press, 1971), p. 158. For a critical view of Myer's role in the internment, see Richard Drinnon, *Keeper of the Concentration Camps: Dillon S. Myer and American Racism* (Berkeley: University of California Press, 1987).

4. Commission on Wartime Relocation and Internment of Civilians, *Personal Justice Denied: Report of the Commission on Wartime Relocation and Internment of Civilians* (Washington, D.C.: Government Printing Office, 1982), p. 185.

5. Audrie Girdner and Anne Loftis, *The Great Betrayal: The Evacuation of the Japanese-Americans during World War II* (Toronto: Macmillan, 1969), pp. 313–14.

6. Ibid., p. 247.

7. Michi Weglyn, *Years of Infamy: The Untold Story of America's Concentration Camps* (New York: Morrow Quill Paperbacks, a division of William Morrow and Company, 1976), p. 145.

8. Wilson and Hosokawa, p. 220.

9. Ernest Yoshida interview, Cortez, Calif., January 24, 1982.

10. Kusaba, Lindley, and McClelland, p. 5.

11. Ibid., p. 6.

12. Ibid., p. 7.

13. U.S. Department of the Interior, War Relocation Authority, *The Evacuated People: A Quantitative Description* (Washington, D.C.: Government Printing Office, 1946), p. 17. . . . The camp population fluctuated a great deal, as people transferred between camps, left for and returned from seasonal work, departed for military service, and left to seek education and work in the East and Midwest.

14. Sam Kuwahara interview, Cortez, Calif., January 25, 1982.

15. Kusaba, Lindley, and McClelland, p. 10.

16. Wilson and Hosokawa, p. 219.

17. *Personal Justice Denied,* p. 174.

18. Kusaba, Lindley, and McClelland, p. 11.

19. For an examination of education in the camps, see Thomas James, *Exile Within: The Schooling of Japanese Americans, 1942–1945* (Cambridge: Harvard University Press, 1987).

20. "Issei, Nisei, Kibei," *Fortune* (April 1944), p. 7; Myer, p. 46.

21. Myer, pp. 40–43.

22. Granada Relocation Center, Agricultural Section, Operations Division, *Historical Report* (Amache, Colo., ca. 1945), p. 1 (published by the Amache Historical Society, Torrance, Calif., in 1978).

23. The Amache Historical Society noted in their republication of the *Historical Report* that there was a great deal of inequity in payment for the Granada/Amache Project land — large companies and owners received generous reimbursement; small private owners received only a pittance.

24. Ibid., p. 1.

25. Ibid., p. 2.

26. Ibid., p. 4.

27. Ibid.

28. Ibid.

29. Letter from June Suzuki to Barbara Carpenter, from Amache, Colo., December 9, 1942; cited by Betty Frances Brown, "The Evacuation of the Japanese Population from a California Agricultural Community," M.A. thesis, Stanford University, 1944, p. 157.

30. Letter from Haruko Kubo to Pat Carpenter, from Amache, Colo., October 4, 1942; cited by Brown, p. 157.

31. Girdner and Loftis, p. 247.

32. Harry H. L. Kitano, *Japanese Americans: The Evolution of a Subculture,* 2nd ed. (Englewood Cliffs, N.J.: Prentice-Hall, 1976), p. 77.

33. Daisuke Kitagawa, *Issei and Nisei: The Internment Years* (New York: Seabury Press, 1967), p. 86.

34. Ibid., pp. 89–90.

35. Ibid., p. 90.

36. Kitano, pp. 75–76.

37. Leonard Bloom, "Familial Adjustments of Japanese-Americans to Relocation: First Phase," *American Sociological Review* 8 (October 1943): 559.

38. Girdner and Loftis, p. 317.

39. Genevieve W. Carter, "Child Care and Youth Problems in a Relocation Center," *Journal of Consulting Psychology* 8 (July–August 1944): 223–24.

40. Eddie Shimano, "Blueprint for a Slum," *Common Ground* 3 (Summer 1943): 81.

41. Carey McWilliams, *North from Mexico: The Spanish-Speaking People of the United States* (New York: Greenwood Press, 1968), pp. 240–41.

42. Ibid., p. 243.

43. *1944 Onlooker,* Foreword.

44. Betty Kanameishi, *1944 Onlooker.*

45. The disastrous consequences of this poorly thought out clearance procedure have been examined in depth by Weglyn, pp. 134–73; Wilson and Hosokawa,

pp. 226–33; Girdner and Loftis, pp. 342–43; and Dorothy S. Thomas and Richard Nishimoto, *The Spoilage: Japanese American Evacuation and Resettlement during World War II* (Berkeley: University of California Press, 1969).

46. Kumekichi Taniguchi interview, Cortez, Calif., January 26, 1982.

47. Weglyn, p. 98.

48. Ibid., p. 101.

49. "Loyalty: Leave and Segregation," in *Personal Justice Denied*, pp. 185–212.

50. Ibid., p. 186.

51. Weglyn, p. 136.

52. Some of the works dealing in depth with resistance within the camps are Roger Daniels, *Concentration Camps USA: Japanese Americans and World War II* (New York: Holt, Rinehart & Winston, 1971); Thomas and Nishimoto, *The Spoilage;* Kitagawa, *Issei and Nisei;* John Okada's novel, *No-No Boy* (Seattle: University of Washington Press, 1979); Gary Y. Okihiro, "Japanese Resistance in America's Concentration Camps: A Re-evaluation," *Amerasia Journal* 2 (1973): 20–34; Arthur A. Hansen and David A. Hacker, "The Manzanar Riot: An Ethnic Perspective," *Amerasia Journal* 2 (Fall 1974): 112–57; Douglas W. Nelson, *Heart Mountain: The History of an American Concentration Camp* (Madison: State Historical Society of Wisconsin for the Department of History, University of Wisconsin, 1976); Brian Masaru Hayashi, "'For the Sake of Our Japanese Brethren': Assimilation, Nationalism, and Protestantism among the Japanese of Los Angeles, 1895–1942," Ph.D. diss., University of California at Los Angeles, 1990.

53. Wilson and Hosokawa, p. 243.

54. Masaharu Ano, "Loyal Linguists: Nisei of World War II Learned Japanese in Minnesota," *Minnesota History* 45 (Fall 1977): 283; Mei Nakano, *Japanese American Women: Three Generations, 1890–1990* (Berkeley: Mina Press, and San Francisco: National Japanese American Historical Society, 1990), p. 170.

55. "Go for Broke" exhibition brochure, Presidio Army Museum, 1981, p. 21; Girdner and Loftis, p. 330.

56. *Personal Justice Denied*, p. 256. For fuller accounts of the 100th and the 442nd, see Masayo Umezawa Duus, *Unlikely Liberators: The Men of the 100th and 442nd*, trans. Peter Duus (Honolulu: University of Hawaii Press, 1983, 1987); and Thomas D. Murphy, *Ambassadors in Arms* (Honolulu: University of Hawaii Press, 1954).

57. *Personal Justice Denied*, p. 256. As Gary Okihiro has helpfully pointed out, a Korean American and several part-Hawaiian men also served in the 100th Battalion.

58. Hiroshi Asai interview, Cortez, Calif., February 23, 1982.

59. "Go for Broke" exhibition brochure, p. 21. The usual regimental complement is 4,500. Given their distinguished record, Hosokawa and Wilson have pointed out that it is strange that only one Nisei received the Medal of Honor. Fifty-two Nisei were awarded the next highest decoration, the Distinguished Service Cross, indicating that a number were recommended for the Medal of Honor and that the recommendations were downgraded. At the end of the war, following a Military Affairs Committee investigation, Pfc. Sadao Munemori — one of 650 who gave their lives — became the only Nisei to win the Medal of Honor in World War II. "Had the men of the 442nd been of a different color," Wilson and Hosokawa ask, "would there have been more Medal of Honor winners?" (p. 240).

60. Noriko Sawada Bridges, "To Be or Not to Be: There's No Such Option," broadside, no date. The experiences of the 442nd find parallel in those of the also segregated Chicano "E" Company of World War II, chronicled in Raul Morin's *Among*

the Valiant: Mexican-Americans in World War II and Korea (Alhambra, Calif.: Borden, 1966).

61. *Personal Justice Denied,* p. 256; for accounts of the Nisei MIS, see Joseph D. Harrington, *Yankee Samurai: The Secret Role of Nisei in America's Pacific Victory* (Detroit, Mich.: Pettigrew, 1979); and Ano, pp. 273–87.

62. Wilson and Hosokawa, pp. 240–41.

63. Harrington, pp. 11–12.

64. Ano, pp. 273–87.

65. Harrington, p. 89; Ano, pp. 277–79.

66. Ano, p. 283.

67. Ibid., p. 287.

68. Kiyoshi Yamamoto interview, Cortez, Calif., February 6, 1982.

69. Ibid.

70. Harrington, p. 87.

71. Kiyoshi Yamamoto interview, Cortez, Calif., February 6, 1982.

72. Ibid.

73. According to educator Robert O'Brien, 4,300 Japanese American students were relocated altogether. Robert O'Brien, *The College Nisei* (Palo Alto, Calif.: Pacific Books, 1949), p. 90.

74. Ibid., p. 135.

75. Mark Kamiya interview, Cortez, Calif., February 8, 1982.

76. O'Brien, p. 74.

77. Mary Noda Kamiya interview, Ballico, Calif., February 13, 1982.

78. Leonard Bloom, "Transitional Adjustments of Japanese-American Families to Relocation," *American Sociological Review* 12 (April 1947): 206.

79. Ibid., p. 208.

80. Leonard Bloom and Ruth Riemer, *Removal and Return: The Socio-Economic Effects of the War on Japanese Americans* (Berkeley: University of California Press, 1949), p. 36.

81. Wilson and Hosokawa, p. 218.

82. Miye Kato Baba interview, Cortez, Calif., July 18, 1982.

83. Ibid.

84. Mary Noda Kamiya interview, Ballico, Calif., February 13, 1982.

85. Florice Morimoto Kuwahara interview, Cortez, Calif., January 25, 1982.

86. Ernest Yoshida interview, Cortez, Calif., January 24, 1982.

87. Wilson and Hosokawa, p. 219.

88. George Yuge interview, Cortez, Calif., February 8, 1982.

89. Ernest Yoshida interview, Cortez, Calif., January 24, 1982.

90. George Yuge interview, Cortez, Calif., February 8, 1982.

91. Wilson and Hosokawa, p. 220.

92. Kitano, p. 75.

93. I have examined the wartime experiences of Nisei women — particularly those who left the camps to seek work and education — in greater detail in an article, "Japanese American Women during World War II," *Frontiers* 8, no. 1 (1984): 6–14.

Making Connections

The questions that precede each selection are intended to help students deal with a particular piece of writing. But all the selections here are in dialogue with one another around one larger problem. That problem is how we can best understand the internment of Japanese Americans during World War II. As the selections show, there are many possibilities for addressing that problem. They may be mutually exclusive. Or they may complement one another. It is certainly the case that each of these selections makes much more sense if read as part of a discussion rather than standing alone. The questions that follow should aid students to realize that the discussion is not finished and that everyone is free to join in.

1. Valerie Matsumoto ends her book by declaring, "Perhaps scholars should be reminded that we, no less than those we study, are actors in history, making choices that affect the lives of others." Do you agree? How would you compare the choices made by these five authors and the impact they can have on the lives of Americans?

2. How might the research agendas and interpretations of these five historians reflect their personal backgrounds, the social movements of the 1960s and 1970s, and their relationships with the Japanese American community?

3. How do these selections shed new light on the history of racism, governmental policy, protest, families, and ethnic communities in America?

4. In the 1970s, the focus of historical research shifted from the architects of internment to the internees. How did this shift change people's understanding of internment?

5. These scholars use a variety of sources — Army transcripts of phone conversations, intelligence reports, office memos, court documents, camp records, and oral histories. Evaluate the strengths and weaknesses of the sources used by each author.

6. In 1981, two surviving architects of internment — Karl Bendetsen and John J. McCloy — tried to defend internment by suggesting that

Japanese Americans were "evacuated" for their own safety and protection. How does the research by Roger Daniels cast doubt on this explanation?

7. How did Peter Irons's research help Minoru Yasui, Gordon Hirabayashi, and Fred Korematsu overturn their wartime convictions?

8. After suing the government, internees from Latin America were offered $5,000 in redress. Could you use Michi Weglyn's research to argue that they deserved the same compensation of $20,000 offered to Japanese American internees?

9. Gary Okihiro argues that internment "is not so much a moral lesson to white America as it is a part of the history of Asians in America." How might this perspective have affected his research and interpretations?

10. Valerie Matsumoto was able to take advantage of the oral history sources that became available in the 1980s. How did such sources change the way people understand internment?

11. Matsumoto calls herself both an insider and an outsider in the Cortez community. She considers herself an insider because her family did agricultural work and was interned. She considers herself an outsider because she did not grow up in a Japanese American community. Compare the value of "insider" and "outsider" relationships to someone conducting oral histories. What might be the advantages and disadvantages of both kinds of relationships?

12. The Civil Liberties Act awarding Japanese Americans redress was passed on August 10, 1988. Over ten years, the government paid $1.6 billion to 81,974 eligible claimants. But many who received redress in the early 1990s have since died. Given the dwindling number of former internees, what questions should historians explore before it's too late? What research agendas should they pursue? In other words, what do we still need to learn about the history of internment?

Suggestions for Further Reading

This volume is not intended to provide a massive bibliography, but any interested student will want to delve into the subject more deeply. For a selection drawn from a book, the best way to start is to go to that book and place the selection within the author's larger argument. Each selection is reproduced with full annotation, as originally published, to allow interested students to go to the author's original sources, study them, and compare their own readings with what the author has made of the same material.

There is a wealth of material on Japanese American history and internment. Students who would like information on the general history of Asian Americans during this period, as well as an overview of internment, should consult Roger Daniels, *Asian America: Chinese and Japanese in the United States since 1850* (Seattle: University of Washington Press, 1988); Sucheng Chan, *Asian Americans: An Interpretive History* (Boston: Twayne Publishers, 1991); and Ronald Takaki, *Strangers from a Different Shore: A History of Asian Americans* (Boston: Little, Brown, 1989). Brian Niiya, ed., *Japanese American History: An A-to-Z Reference from 1868 to the Present* (Los Angeles: Japanese American National Museum, 1993), provides many entries on internment and other historical experiences and includes Gary Y. Okihiro's essay "The Japanese in America," summarizing all of Japanese American history. Roger Daniels gives a concise review of prewar racism, internment, and redress in *Prisoners without Trial: Japanese Americans in World War II* (New York: Hill and Wang, 1993). Multiple views of Japanese American experiences before, during, and after the war can be found in Roger Daniels, Sandra C. Taylor, and Harry H. L. Kitano, eds., *Japanese Americans: From Relocation to Redress* (Salt Lake City: University of Utah Press, 1986). An overview of the prewar anti-Japanese movement can be found in Roger Daniels, *The Politics of Prejudice: The Anti-Japanese Movement in California and the Struggle for Japanese Exclusion* (Berkeley and Los Angeles: University of California Press, 1962). John Dower, *War without Mercy: Race and Power in the Pacific War* (New York: Pantheon Books, 1986), compares racial stereotyping on both sides of the Pacific during World War II. Social psychologist Harry H. L. Kitano provides an early examination of Japanese American culture and community in *Japanese Americans: The Evolution of a Subculture,* 2nd ed. (Englewood Cliffs, N.J.: Prentice Hall, 1976); Jere Takahashi revises Kitano's analysis and extends his study to the third generation in *Nisei/Sansei: Shifting Japanese American Identities and Politics* (Philadelphia: Temple University Press, 1997).

To understand the causes of the decision to intern Japanese Americans, students should first review the official (and mendacious) rationale presented in U.S. Department of War, *Final Report: Japanese Evacuation from the West Coast, 1942* (Washington, D.C.: Government Printing Office, 1943). Contemporary critiques of this rationale are offered by Carey McWilliams, *Prejudice: Japanese Americans, Symbols of Racial Intolerance* (Boston: Little, Brown, 1944) and *What about Our Japanese Americans?* (New York: Public Affairs Committee, 1944). Eugene Rostow also attacks the decision in two articles, "The Japanese American Cases — A Disaster," *Yale Law Journal* 54 (1945): 489–533, and "Our Worst Wartime Mistake," *Harper's,* 191 (1945): 193–201. Morton Grodzins denounces the West Coast politicians, press, and economic groups that advocated internment in *Americans Betrayed: Politics and the Japanese Evacuation* (Chicago: University of Chicago Press, 1949). Jacobus tenBroek, Edward N. Barnhart, and Floyd M. Matson challenge Grodzins's analysis of the role of West Coast groups and emphasize DeWitt's responsibility in *Prejudice, War, and the Constitution* (Berkeley and Los Angeles: University of California Press, 1954). The authoritative historical account of the decision, excerpted here, is still Roger Daniels, *Concentration Camps, USA: Japanese Americans and World War II* (New York: Holt, Rinehart & Winston, 1971). Daniels revised this account and includes a comparison of policies toward Japanese Canadians in *Concentration Camps, North America: Japanese in the United States and Canada during World War II* (Malabar, Fla.: Krieger Publishing, 1981). Daniels also provides nine volumes of primary sources on policy development in *American Concentration Camps* (New York: Garland, 1989). The book that had the most influence on the Japanese American community's views of the government and internment, excerpted here, is Michi Weglyn, *Years of Infamy: The Untold Story of America's Concentration Camps* (New York: Morrow Quill Paperbacks, a Division of Morrow and Company, 1976). Gordon Hirabayashi's experiences, also described here, can be found in Peter Irons, ed., *The Courage of Their Convictions* (New York: The Free Press, 1988). A more detailed account of the government's misrepresentation of evidence before the Supreme Court in the Hirabayashi, Yasui, and Korematsu cases is presented in Peter Irons, *Justice at War: The Story of the Japanese American Internment Cases* (New York: Oxford University Press, 1983). Peter Irons, ed., *Justice Delayed: The Record of the Japanese American Internment Cases* (Middletown, Conn.: Wesleyan University Press, 1989), provides transcripts of the Hirabayashi, Yasui, and Korematsu trials, with an introduction summarizing the *coram nobis* cases.

Self-serving views of the "positive" aspects of camp life are promoted in War Relocation Authority, *WRA: The Story of Human Conservation* (Washington, D.C.: Government Printing Office, 1946); and Dillon S. Myer, *Uprooted Americans: The Japanese Americans and the War Relocation Authority during World War II* (Tucson: University of Arizona Press, 1971). Histories by the "community analysts" in camp include Alexander H. Leighton, *The Governing of Men: General Principles and Recommendations Based on Experience at a Japanese Relocation Camp* (Princeton: Princeton University Press, 1945); and Edward H. Spicer, Asael T. Hansen, Katherine Luomala, and Marvin K. Opler, *Impounded People: Japanese-Americans in the Relocation Centers* (Tucson: University of Arizona Press, 1969). Orin Starn analyzes the role of these community analysts in "Engineering Internment: Anthropologists and the War Relocation Authority," *American Ethnologist* 13, no. 4 (1986): 700–720. For more revisionist works that emphasize the injustice of the decision and suffering within the camps, see Audrie Girdner and Anne Loftis, *The Great Betrayal: The Evacuation of the Japanese-Americans during World War II* (Toronto: Macmillan, 1969); and Alan R. Bosworth, *America's Concentration Camps* (New York: Norton, 1967). Former internee and activist Raymond Okamura denounces terms such as *evacuation* and *relocation centers* in "The American Concentration Camps: A Cover-Up through Euphemistic Terminology," *Journal of Ethnic Studies* 10, no. 3 (Fall 1982): 95–109. For a searing denunciation of the paternalism of the WRA's director, see Richard Drinnon, *Keeper of Concentration Camps: Dillon S. Myer and American Racism* (Berkeley and Los Angeles: University of California Press, 1987). One of the few recent works to defend the WRA from charges of racism is Page Smith, *Democracy on Trial: The Japanese American Evacuation and Relocation in World War II* (New York: Simon & Schuster, 1995).

Numerous studies focus on individual camps. These works include Sandra C. Taylor, *Jewel of the Desert: Japanese American Internment at Topaz* (Berkeley: University of California Press, 1993); Leonard J Arrington, *The Price of Prejudice: The Japanese-American Relocation Center in Utah during World War II* (Logan: Faculty Association, Utah State University, 1962); Paul Dayton Bailey, *City in the Sun: The Japanese Concentration Camp at Poston, Arizona* (Los Angeles: Westernlore Press, 1971); and Anthony L. Lehman, *Birthright of Barbed Wire: The Santa Anita Assembly Center for the Japanese* (Los Angeles: Westernlore Press, 1970). Jessie A. Garrett and Ronald C. Larson, eds., *Camp and Community: Manzanar and the Owens Valley* (Fullerton: Japanese American Project of the Oral History Program, California State University at Fullerton, 1977), includes interviews with non–Japanese American residents who lived near Manzanar. For an account of Tule Lake from a JERS perspective, see Dorothy Thomas and Richard S. Nishimoto, *The Spoilage: Japanese American Evacuation and Resettlement during World War II* (Berkeley: University of California Press, 1946). Yuji Ichioka, ed., *Views from Within: The Japanese American Evacuation and Resettlement Study* (Los Angeles: Asian American Studies Center, University of California at Los Angeles, 1989), contains reflections and critiques of the JERS research. Lane Ryo Hirabayashi critically analyzes the ethics and politics of ethnographic fieldwork by examining the experiences of Tamie Tsuchiyama, the only professionally trained Japanese American female JERS researcher, in *The Politics of Fieldwork: Research in an American Concentration Camp* (Tucson: University of Arizona Press, 1999). Peter Suzuki denounces the practices of the community analysts and JERS researchers in "Anthropologists in the Wartime Camps for Japanese Americans: A Documentary Study," *Dialectical Anthropology* 6, no. 1 (August 1981): 23–60, and "The University of California Japanese Evacuation and Resettlement Study: A Prolegomenon," *Dialectical Anthropology* 10 (1986): 189–213. For the views of individual JERS researchers, see Charles Kikuchi, *The Kikuchi Diary: Chronicle from an American Concentration Camp, the Tanforan Journals of Charles Kikuchi*, ed. John Modell (Urbana: University of Illinois Press, 1973); Richard S. Nishimoto, *Inside an American Concentration Camp: Japanese American Resistance at Poston, Arizona*, ed. Lane Ryo Hirabayashi (Tucson: University of Arizona Press, 1995); and Rosalie H. Wax, *Doing Fieldwork: Warnings and Advice* (Chicago and London: University of Chicago Press, 1971).

Early accounts of Japanese American responses to internment were written by the Japanese American Citizens League. JACL leader Bill Hosokowa, *Nisei: The Quiet Americans* (New York: William Morrow, 1969), emphasizes the experiences of internees who "proved" their loyalty on the battlefield. Hosokowa's *JACL: In Quest of Justice, History of the Japanese American Citizens League* (New York: William Morrow, 1982) provides an insider's account of the JACL's history. JACL leader Mike Masaoka's memoir, *They Call Me Moses Masaoka: An American Saga* (New York: William Morrow, 1987), also defends JACL cooperation during the war and praises JACL achievements in the postwar period. Yuji Ichioka, "A Study in Dualism: James Yoshinori Sakamoto and the Japanese American Courier, 1928–1942," *Amerasia Journal* 13, no. 2 (1986–1987): 49–81, analyzes the attitudes of an important JACL leader. Bob Kumamoto, "The Search for Spies: American Counterintelligence and the Japanese American Community, 1931–42," *Amerasia Journal* 6, no. 2 (1979): 45–75, reveals evidence of JACL informing on immigrant leaders in the decade before Pearl Harbor. Paul Spickard, "The Nisei Assume Power: The Japanese Citizens League, 1941–1942," *Pacific Historical Review* 52, no. 2 (May 1983): 147–74, notes JACL attempts to replace Issei leaders, promote military service and assimilation, and suppress camp protest during the war. Kevin Allen Leonard shows how the JACL used patriotic images to undermine anti-Japanese legislation after the war in "'Is That What We Fought For?' Japanese Americans and Racism in California: The Impact of World War II," *Western Historical Quarterly* 21, no. 4 (November 1990): 463–82. Accounts of Japanese Americans who served in the armed forces include Joseph D. Harrington, *Yankee Samurai: The Secret Role of Nisei in America's Pacific Victory* (Detroit: Pettigrew Enterprises, 1979); Masayo Duus, *Unlikely Liberators: The Men of the 100th and the 442nd* (Honolulu: University of Hawaii Press, 1987); Thelma Chang, *"I Can Never Forget": Men of the 100th/442nd* (Honolulu: Sigi Productions, 1991); Lyn Crost, *Honor by Fire: Japanese Americans at War in Europe and the Pacific* (Novato, Calif.: Presidio Press, 1994); Chester Tanaka, *Go for Broke: A Pictorial History of the Japanese American 100th Infantry and the 442nd Regimental Combat Team* (Richmond, Calif.: Go for Broke, 1981); Tad Ichinokuchi, ed., *John Aiso and the M.I.S.: Japanese-American Soldiers in the Military Intelligence Service, World War II* (Los Angeles: Military Intelligence Service Club of Southern California, 1988); and Tamotsu Shibutani, *The Derelicts of Company K: A Sociological Study of Demoralization* (Berkeley and Los Angeles: University of California Press, 1978).

In the 1970s, researchers reexamined the history of resistance in the camps. Gary Y. Okihiro's study of Tule Lake under martial law is included in this collection. Other articles by Okihiro include "Japanese Resistance in America's Concentration Camps: A Re-evaluation," *Amerasia Journal* 2, no. 1 (1973): 20–34; and "Religion and Resistance in America's Concentration Camps," *Phylon* 45, no. 3 (September 1984): 220–33. The other seminal work on resistance is Arthur A. Hansen and David A. Hacker, "The Manzanar Riot: An Ethnic Perspective," *Amerasia Journal* 2, no. 2 (Fall 1974): 112–57. Hansen also provides an insightful analysis in "Cultural Politics in the Gila River Relocation Center, 1942–1943," *Arizona and the West* 27 (Winter 1985): 327–62. A firsthand account of Manzanar by the man whose arrest sparked the riot can be found in Sue Kunitomi Embrey, Arthur A. Hansen, and Betty Mitson, eds., *Manzanar Martyr: An Interview with Harry A. Ueno* (Fullerton: Japanese American Project of the Oral History Program, California State University at Fullerton, 1986). For a contrasting view, see Karl G. Yoneda, *Ganbatte! The Sixty-Year Struggle of a Kibei Worker* (Los Angeles: Asian American Studies Center, University of California at Los Angeles, 1983). Draft resistance at Heart Mountain is discussed in great detail in Douglas W. Nelson, *Heart Mountain: The History of an American Concentration Camp* (Madison: State Historical Society of Wisconsin, 1976). Firsthand recollections are provided by draft resister Frank Emi, "Draft Resistance at the Heart Mountain Concentration Camp and the Fair Play Committee," in *Frontiers of Asian American Studies: Writing, Research, and Commentary,* ed. Gail M. Nomura et al.

(Pullman: Washington State University Press, 1989); and James Omura, a journalist who supported draft resistance, "Japanese American Journalism during World War II," in *Frontiers of Asian American Studies: Writing, Research, and Commentary*, ed. Gail M. Nomura et al. (Pullman: Washington State University Press, 1989). Arthur A. Hansen interviewed Omura for "James Matsumoto Omura: An Interview," *Amerasia Journal* 13, no. 2 (1986–1987): 99–113. The experiences of the renunciants are reexamined in Donald E. Collins, *Native American Aliens: Disloyalty and the Renunciation of Citizenship by Japanese Americans during World War II* (Westport, Conn.: Greenwood Press, 1985).

Valerie J. Matsumoto, *Farming the Home Place: A Japanese American Community in California, 1919–1982* (Ithaca, N.Y.: Cornell University Press, 1993), excerpted here, examines the impact of internment on families and gender roles. Other works that look at the experiences of women include Valerie Matsumoto, "Japanese American Women during World War II," *Frontiers* 8, no. 1 (1984): 6–14; Mei Nakano, *Japanese American Women: Three Generations, 1890–1990* (Berkeley, Calif.: Mina Publishing Press, and San Francisco: National Japanese American Historical Society, 1990); Dana Takagi, "Personality and History: Hostile Nisei Women," in *Reflections on Shattered Windows: Promises and Prospects for Asian American Studies*, ed. Gary Y. Okihiro et al. (Pullman: Washington State University Press, 1988); Evelyn Nakano Glenn, *Issei, Nisei, War Bride: Three Generations of Japanese American Women in Domestic Service* (Philadelphia: Temple University Press, 1986); and Sylvia Junko Yanagisako, *Transforming the Past: Tradition and Kinship among Japanese Americans* (Stanford, Calif.: Stanford University Press, 1985). For more information on family life, consult John Modell, "The Japanese American Family," *Pacific Historical Review* 37 (1968): 78–79; and Leonard Bloom and John I. Kitsuse, *The Managed Casualty: The Japanese-American Family in World War II*, Culture and Society, vol. 6 (Berkeley: University of California Press, 1956). The best study of educational policies within the camps is Thomas James, *Exile Within: The Schooling of Japanese Americans, 1942–1945* (Cambridge: Harvard University Press, 1987). Information on the experiences of college students can be found in Gary Y. Okihiro, *Storied Lives: Japanese American Students and World War II* (Seattle: University of Washington Press, 1999).

Although there are many studies of the WRA camps, literature on the Department of Justice camps is sparse. Michi Weglyn, *Years of Infamy*, excerpted here, provides an early exposé of the plight of Japanese Latin Americans. For more information on the internment of Peruvians, see C. Harvey Gardiner, *Pawns in a Triangle of Hate: The Peruvian Japanese and the United States* (Seattle: University of Washington Press, 1981). The experiences of Japanese, Italian, and German "alien" internees are discussed in John Christgau, *"Enemies": World War II Alien Internment* (Ames: Iowa State University Press,

1985). More information on Italian American internees can be found in Stephen Fox, *The Unknown Internment: An Oral History of the Relocation of Italian Americans during World War II* (Boston: G. K. Hall, 1990). The voices of Hawaiian internees are prominent in Gary Y. Okihiro, *Cane Fires: The Anti-Japanese Movement in Hawaii, 1865–1945* (Philadelphia: Temple University Press, 1991).

Researchers have only started to explore the history of Japanese Americans in Japan during the war. Most of these works focus on the life of Iva Toguri, who was convicted of treason as "Tokyo Rose" during the war and then pardoned in the 1970s. See Masayo Umezawa Duus, *Tokyo Rose: Orphan of the Pacific* (New York: Kodansha International, 1979); Stanley I. Kutler, "Forging a Legend: The Treason of 'Tokyo Rose,'" *Wisconsin Law Review* 6 (1980): 1341–82; David A. Ward, "The Unending War of Iva Ikuko Toguri D'Aquino: The Trial and Conviction of 'Tokyo Rose,'" *Amerasia Journal* 1, no. 2 (1971): 26–35; Raymond Okamura, "Iva Ikuko Toguri: Victim of an American Fantasy," in *Counterpoint: Perspectives on Asian America,* ed. Emma Gee (Los Angeles: Asian American Studies Center, University of California at Los Angeles, 1976); and Clifford I. Uyeda, "The Pardoning of 'Tokyo Rose': A Report on the Restoration of American Citizenship to Iva Ikuko Toguri," *Amerasia Journal* 5, no. 2 (1978): 69–72. John Stephan, *Hawaii under the Rising Sun: Japan's Plans for Conquest after Pearl Harbor* (Honolulu: University of Hawaii Press, 1984), profiles several Issei who spent World War II in Japan. Firsthand accounts by Nisei who lived in Japan during the war can be found in Mary Tomita, *Dear Miye: Letters Home from Japan, 1939–1946,* ed. Robert G. Lee (Stanford, Calif.: Stanford University Press, 1995); and Jim Yoshida and Bill Hosokowa, *The Two Worlds of Jim Yoshida* (New York: William Morrow, 1972). The life of a Nisei who died while serving against his will in the Japanese army is described in Floyd C. Watkins, "Even His Name Will Die: The Last Days of Paul Nobuo Tatsuguchi," *Journal of Ethnic Studies* 3, no. 4 (Winter 1976): 37–48. Yuji Ichioka examines a Nisei who willingly served in the Japanese army in "The Meaning of Loyalty: The Case of Kazumaro Buddy Uno," *Amerasia Journal* 23, no. 3 (Winter 1997–1998): 45–71. Brian Masaru Hayashi, *"For the Sake of Our Japanese Brethren": Assimilation, Nationalism, and Protestantism among the Japanese of Los Angeles, 1895–1942* (Stanford, Calif.: Stanford University Press, 1995), discusses two Japanese American Protestants who served in the Japanese military during World War II and documents Issei nationalist support for Japan during the war.

Dorothy Thomas, *The Salvage: Japanese American Evacuation and Resettlement during World War II* (Berkeley: University of California Press, 1952), still provides a useful starting point for the study of internees' views of leaving the camps and resettling in the Midwest. The study's bias against individuals affiliated with ethnic groups can be corrected by examining Stephen S.

Fujita and David J. O'Brien, *Japanese American Ethnicity: The Persistence of Community* (Seattle: University of Washington Press, 1991). Other useful studies of resettlement include Leonard Bloom and Ruth Riemer, *Removal and Return: The Socio-Economic Effects of the War on Japanese Americans,* Culture and Society, vol. 4 (Berkeley: University of California Press, 1949); Mitziko Sawada, "After the Camps: Seabrook Farms, New Jersey, and the Resettlement of Japanese Americans, 1944–47," *Amerasia Journal* 13, no. 2 (1986–1987): 117–36; and two articles by Sandra C. Taylor, "Japanese Americans and Keetley Farms: Utah's Relocation Colony," *Utah Historical Quarterly* 54, no. 4 (Fall 1986): 328–44, and "Leaving the Concentration Camps: Japanese American Resettlement in Utah and the Intermountain West," *Pacific Historical Review* 60, no. 2 (May 1991): 169–94. Memories of the resettlement experience are recounted in Brian Niiya et al., eds., *Nanka Nikkei Voices: Resettlement Years, 1945–1955* (Los Angeles: Japanese American Historical Society of Southern California, 1999); Tetsuden Kashima addresses internees' suppression of memories of the war in "Japanese American Internees Return, 1945 to 1955: Readjustment and Social Amnesia," *Phylon* 41, no. 2 (Summer 1980): 107–15. Donna K. Nagata explores internees' unconscious transmission of trauma to their children in *Legacy of Injustice: Exploring the Cross-Generational Impact of the Japanese American Internment* (New York and London: Plenum Press, 1993). Don Nakanishi analyzes the resurrection of these suppressed memories of internment in "Seeking Convergence in Race Relations Research: Japanese-Americans and the Resurrection of Internment," in *Eliminating Racism,* ed. Phyllis A. Katz and Dalmas A. Taylor (New York and London: Plenum Press, 1988), and "Surviving Democracy's Mistake: Japanese Americans and the Enduring of Executive Order 9066," *Amerasia Journal* 19, no. 1 (1993): 37–60. Arthur A. Hansen notes the impact of redress on attitudes about oral history in "Oral History and the Japanese American Evacuation," *Journal of American History* 82, no. 2 (September 1995): 625–39.

A growing number of works examine the history of the redress movement. Edited transcripts of Japanese American testimony during the 1981 Commission on Wartime Relocation and Internment of Civilians hearings are included in "Testimonies to the Commission on Wartime Relocation and Internment of Civilians," *Amerasia Journal* 8, no. 2 (Fall/Winter 1981): 55–105. The commission's historical report, which concludes that the decision to intern Japanese Americans was the result of "race prejudice, war hysteria, and a failure of political leadership," was published as *Personal Justice Denied: Report of the Commission on Wartime Relocation and Internment of Civilians* (Washington, D.C.: Government Printing Office, 1982). William Minoru Hohri, *Repairing America: An Account of the Movement for Japanese-American Redress* (Pullman: Washington State University Press, 1984), recounts the struggle of the National Council for Japanese American Redress to sue the government. Yasuko Takezawa, *Breaking the Silence: Redress and Japanese American Ethnicity* (Ithaca, N.Y.: Cornell University Press, 1995), documents the history of the redress movement in Seattle. Leslie Hatamiya, *Righting a Wrong: Japanese Americans and the Passage of the Civil Liberties Act of 1988* (Stanford, Calif.: Stanford University Press, 1993), examines the battle for legislative redress. Lillian Baker, a former hat pin collector and columnist, denounces the revisionist scholarship and the movement for redress in *Concentration Camp Conspiracy: A Second Pearl Harbor* (Lawndale, Calif.: Americans for Historical Accuracy Publications, 1981).

Early firsthand accounts by internees include the drawings and captions in Mine Okubo, *Citizen 13660* (New York: Columbia University Press, 1946), and Monica Sone, *Nisei Daughter* (Seattle: University of Washington Press, 1953). The list of firsthand accounts mushroomed during the 1970s to include Yoshiko Uchida, *Journey to Topaz: A Story of the Japanese American Evacuation* (New York: Charles Scribner's Sons, 1971); Jeanne Wakatsuki Houston and James D. Houston, *Farewell to Manzanar: A True Story of Japanese-American Experience during and after World War II Internment* (Boston: Houghton Mifflin, 1973); Jack Matsuoka, *Camp II, Block 211: Daily Life in an Internment Camp* (San Francisco: Japan Publications, 1974); Takeo Kaneshiro, comp., *Internees: War Relocation Center Memoirs and Diaries* (New York: Vantage Press, 1976); James Oda, *Heroic Struggles of Japanese Americans: Partisan Fighters from America's Concentration Camps* (KNI, 1981); Kiyo Hirano, *Enemy Alien,* trans. George Hirano and Yuri Kageyama (San Francisco: Japantown Art and Media Workshop, 1984); Robert S. Yasui, *Yasui Family of Hood River, Oregon,* ed. Holly Yasui (N.p.: Holly Yasui, 1987); Mary Tsukamoto and Elizabeth Pinkerton, *We the People: A Story of Internment in America* (Elk Grove, Calif.: Laguna Publishers, 1988); Reverend Yoshiaki Fukuda, *My Six Years of Internment: An Issei's Struggle for Justice* (San Francisco: Konko Church, 1990; translation of *Yokuryu Seikatsu Rokunen,* Okayama, Japan: Tamashima Kappansho, 1957); and Yamato Ichihashi, *Morning Glory, Evening Shadow: Yamato Ichihashi and His Internment Writings, 1942–1945,* ed. Gordon H. Chang (Stanford, Calif.: Stanford University Press, 1997).

More researchers began collecting oral histories in the 1970s. Arthur A. Hansen and Betty E. Mitson, eds., *Voices Long Silent: An Oral Inquiry into the Japanese-American Evacuation* (Fullerton: Japanese American Project of the Oral History Program, California State University at Fullerton, 1974), is a pioneering collection of interviews. Arthur A. Hansen also edited a five-part, six-volume collection of oral histories of internees, administrators, analysts, resisters, guards, and townspeople titled *Japanese American World War II Evacuation Oral History Project* (Westport, Conn.: Meckler, 1991; Munich: K. G. Saur, 1993–1995). Oral histories of Japanese American immigrants can be found in Kazuo Ito, *Issei: A History of Japanese Immigrants in North America,* trans. Shinichiro Nakamura and Jean S. Gerard (Seattle: Executive Committee for the Publication of Issei, 1973); and Eileen Sunada Sarasohn, ed., *The Issei: Portrait of a Pioneer* (Palo Alto, Calif.: Pacific Books, 1983). John Tateishi, *And Justice for All: An Oral History of the Japanese American Detention Camps* (New York: Random House, 1984), contains diverse views and experiences of internment. Anthropologist Akemi Kikumura explores the experiences of her mother and father in *Through Harsh Winters: The Life of a Japanese Immigrant Woman* (Novato, Calif.: Chandler & Sharp Publishers, 1981) and *Promises Kept: The Life of an Issei Man* (Novato, Calif.: Chandler & Sharp Publishers, 1991). Finally, for photographs of camp life, see Ansel E. Adams, *Born Free and Equal: Photographs of the Loyal Japanese-Americans at Manzanar Relocation Center* (New York: U.S. Camera, 1944); and Ansel E. Adams and Toyo Miyatake, *Two Views of Manzanar: An Exhibition of Photographs* (Los Angeles: Frederick S. Wright Art Gallery, University of California at Los Angeles, 1978). For photographs and an essay on the remains of the ten WRA camps, see *Whispered Silences: Japanese Americans and World War II,* photographs by Joan Myers, essay by Gary Y. Okihiro (Seattle: University of Washington Press, 1996).

Acknowledgments, continued from p. ii.

Truman's eighth Presidential Distinguished Unit Citation to the 100/442nd.
Photograph from the archives of the National Japanese American Historical
Society, 1684 Post Street, San Francisco, CA 94115, used with permission.

ROGER DANIELS, "The Decision for Mass Evacuation," from *Concentration Camps
USA: Japanese Americans and World War II* by Roger Daniels (New York: Holt,
Rinehart & Winston, 1971), 42–73. Reprinted by permission of Roger Daniels.

PETER IRONS, "*Gordon Hirabayashi v. United States:* 'A Jap's a Jap,'" from *The
Courage of Their Convictions* by Peter Irons (New York: The Free Press, 1988),
39–49. Reprinted by permission of The Free Press, a Division of Simon and
Schuster, Inc.

VALERIE J. MATSUMOTO, "Amache," from *Farming the Home Place: A Japanese American
Community in California, 1919–1982.* Copyright © 1993 by Cornell University.
Used by permission of Cornell University Press.

GARY Y. OKIHIRO, "Tule Lake under Martial Law: A Study in Japanese Resistance,"
from *Journal of Ethnic Studies* 5, no. 3 (Fall 1977): 71–85. Reprinted by
permission of the author.

MICHI WEGLYN, "Hostages," from *Years of Infamy: The Untold Story of America's
Concentration Camps* by Michi Weglyn (New York: Morrow Quill Paperbacks,
a Division of William Morrow and Company, Inc., 1976), 54–66 and 285–89.
Reprinted by permission of California State Polytechnic University, Pomona.